STUDIES OF THE STAGE

Brander Matthews

STUDIES OF
THE STAGE

BY

BRANDER MATTHEWS

Essay Index Reprint Series

BOOKS FOR LIBRARIES PRESS
FREEPORT, NEW YORK

First Published 1894
Reprinted 1972

Library of Congress Cataloging in Publication Data

Matthews, Brander, 1852-1929.
    Studies of the stage.

    (Essay index reprint series)
    Reprint of the 1894 ed.
    CONTENTS: The dramatization of novels.--The
dramatic outlook in America.--The players. [etc.]
    1. Drama--Addresses, essays, lectures. 2. Theater
--Addresses, essays, lectures. I. Title.
PN1657.M3 1972   809.2   72-294
ISBN 0-8369-2806-7

PRINTED IN THE UNITED STATES OF AMERICA
BY
NEW WORLD BOOK MANUFACTURING CO., INC.
HALLANDALE, FLORIDA 33009

*To AGNES ETHEL, who once adorned
the Stage for an all too brief period, these
Studies are inscribed by her friend of
many years, the AUTHOR*

PREFATORY NOTE

THESE essays upon theatrical subjects differ from most other papers about plays and playwrights, mainly because of the writer's different point of view. While the theatrical critic in general looks at the drama from his seat in the orchestra, my standpoint has always been the stage itself. Being, for my own part, a maker of plays, I have considered the art of the dramatist with a fuller understanding of its technic, I hope, and with a more intimate sympathy, I think, than is possible to those who know the stage only from the far side of the footlights. In fact, I am quite willing to have this little volume considered as an argument in favor of the contention that dramatic literature must approve itself as drama first, before it need be discussed as literature.

B. M.

COLUMBIA COLLEGE,
  February, 1894.

CONTENTS

THE DRAMATIZATION OF NOVELS

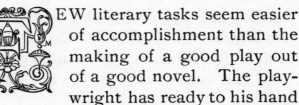

EW literary tasks seem easier of accomplishment than the making of a good play out of a good novel. The playwright has ready to his hand a story, a sequence of situations, a group of characters artfully contrasted, the suggestion of the requisite scenery, and occasional passages of appropriate conversation. What more is needed than a few sheets of paper and a pair of scissors, a pen and a little plodding patience? The pecuniary reward is abundant; apparently the feat is temptingly facile; and every year we see many writers succumb to the temptation. Whenever a novel hits the popular fancy and is seen for a season in everybody's hands, be it *Mr. Barnes of New York* or *She*, *The Quick or the Dead?* or *Robert Elsmere*, the adapter steps forward and sets the

story on the stage, counting on the reflected reputation of the novel to attract
the public to witness the play. But the
result of the calculation is rarely satisfactory, and the dramatized romance is rarely successful. Frequently it is an instant
failure, like the recent perversion of *Robert Elsmere ;* occasionally it is forced into
a fleeting popularity by managerial wiles,
like the stage versions of *She* and *Mr.
Barnes of New York ;* and only now and
again is it really welcomed by the public,
like the dramatizations of *Little Lord
Fauntleroy* and *Uncle Tom's Cabin.* So
it is that, if we look back along the lists
of plays which have had prolonged popularity, we shall find the titles of very few
dramatizations, and we shall discover that
those which chance to linger in our memory are recalled chiefly because of a for-
tuitous association with the fame of a
favorite actor ; thus the semi - operatic
version of *Guy Mannering* brings before
us Charlotte Cushman's weird embodi-
ment of Meg Merrilies, just as the artless
adaptation of the *Gilded Age* evokes the
joyous humor of John T. Raymond as

Colonel Sellers. And if we were to make out a list of novels which have been adapted to the stage in the past thirty years or so, we should discover a rarely broken record of overwhelming disaster.

The reason of this is not far to seek. It is to be found in the fundamental difference between the art of the drama and the art of prose - fiction — a difference which the adapter has generally ignored or been ignorant of. Perhaps it is not unfair to suggest that the methods of the dramatist and of the novelist are as unlike as the methods of the sculptor and of the painter. The difference between the play and the novel is at bottom the difference between a precise and rigid form, and a form of almost unlimited range and flexibility. The drama has laws as unbending as those of the sonnet, while the novel may extend itself to the full license of an epic. It is hardly too much to say that nowadays the novelist has complete freedom in choice of subject and in method of treatment. He may be concise or he may be prolix. He may lay the scene of his story in a desert, and find his effect in the slow analysis of a single human soul in awful solitude; or he may create a regiment of characters which shall perform intricate evolutions and move in serried ranks through the crowded streets of a busy city. He may riot in the great phenomena of nature, forcing the tornado, the gale at sea, the plunge of a cataract, the purple sunset after a midsummer storm, to create his catastrophe or to typify some mood of his hero. He may be a persistent pessimist, believing that all is for the worst in the worst of all possible worlds, and painting his fellow-man in harsh black-and-white, with a most moderate use of the white. He may be a philosopher, using a thin veil of fiction as a transparent mask for the exposition of his system of life. He may adopt the novel as a platform or as a pulpit; he may use it as a means or he may accept it as an end; he may do with it what he will; and if he be a man to whom the world wishes to listen or a man who has really something to say, he gains a hearing.

In contrast with the license of the novelist the limitations of the dramatist were

never more distinct than they are to-day.
As the playwright appeals to the play-
goer, he is confined to those subjects in
which the broad public can be interested
and to the treatment which the broad
public will accept. While the writer of
romance may condense his work into a
short story of a column or two, or expand
it to a stout·tome of a thousand pages,
the writer for the stage has no such
choice; his work must be bulky enough
to last from half-past eight to half-past
ten at the shortest, or at the longest from
eight to eleven. In the present condition of the theatre in Great Britain and
the United States, there is little or no
demand for the comedietta or for the
two‑act comedy; a play must be long
enough and strong enough to furnish
forth the whole evening's entertainment.
The dramatist may divide his piece into
three, or four, or five acts, as he may pre-
fer, but except from some good and sufficient reason, there must be but a single
scene to each act. The characters must
be so many in number that no one shall
seem unduly obtrusive; they must be

sharply contrasted; most of them must be sympathetic to the spectators, for the audience in a theatre, however pessimistic it may be individually, is always optimistic as a whole. There must be an infusion of humor at recurrent intervals, and a slowly increasing intensity of emotional stress. In short, the fetters of the dramatist are as obvious as is the freedom of the novelist.

Perhaps the chief disadvantage under which the dramatist labors is that it is almost impossible for him to show adequately the progressive and wellnigh imperceptible disintegration of character under the attrition of recurring circumstance. Time and space are both beyond the control of the maker of plays, while the story-teller may take his hero by slow stages to the world's end. The drama has but five acts at most, and the theatre is but a few yards wide. Description is scarcely permissible in a play; and it may be the most beautiful and valuable part of a novel. Comment by the author is absolutely impossible on the stage; and there are many who love certain novels—

Thackeray's for example—chiefly because they feel therein the personal presence of the author. It is at once the merit and the difficulty of dramatic art that the characters must reveal themselves; they must be illuminated from within, not from without; they must speak for themselves in unmistakable terms; and the author cannot dissect them for us or lay bare their innermost thoughts with his pen as with a scalpel. The drama must needs be synthetic, while now the novel, more often than not, is analytic. The vocabulary of the playwright must be clear, succinct, precise, and picturesque, while that of the novelist may be archaic, fantastic, subtle, or allusive. Simplicity and directness are the ear-marks of a good play; but we all know good novels which are complex, involute, tortuous. A French critic has declared that the laws of the drama are Logic and Movement, by which he means that in a good play the subject clearly exposed at first moves forward by regular steps, artfully prepared, straight to its inevitable end.

After all, art is but a question of selection: no man can put the whole of life either on the stage or into a book. He must choose the facts which seem to him salient and which will best serve his purpose. He must reject unhesitatingly all the others, as valuable in themselves, it may be, but foreign to the work in hand. The principles differ which govern this selection by the dramatist and by the novelist. Details which are insignificant in a story may be of the greatest value in a play ; and effects of prime importance in the tale may be contrary to the practice of the playwright, or even physically impossible on the stage. George Sand was a great novelist who was passionately occupied with the theatre, although she was wholly without the dramatic gift ; and in his biographical study of her career and her character the late M. Caro noted her constant failure as a dramatist, both with original plays and with adaptations of her own novels, declaring in these words the reason of this failure : " What is needed on the stage is the art of relief, the instinct of perspective, adroitness of combination, and, above all, action, again action, and always action. It is natural and laughter-forcing gayety, or the secret of powerful emotion, or the unexpectedness which grips the attention "—all qualities which George Sand lacked.

A mere sequence of *tableaux vivants*, even if it include the characters and present the situations of a successful tale, is not necessarily a successful play, and certainly it is not a good play. It is easy enough to scissor a panorama of scenes from a story, but to make over the story itself into a play is not so easy. To get a true play out of a novel, the dramatist must translate the essential idea from the terms of narrative into the terms of the drama. He must disengage the fundamental subject from the accidental incidents with which the novelist has presented it. He must strip it to the skeleton, and then he must clothe these bare bones with new flesh and fresh muscle in accordance with the needs of the theatre. He must disentangle the primary action and set this on the stage, clearly and simply. To do this it may be necessary to modify characters, to alter the sequence of scenes, to simplify motives, to condense, to clarify, to heighten. The more famous the novel—one might almost say the better the novel—the less likely is it to make a good play, because there is then a greater difficulty in disengaging the main theme from its subsidiary developments; and even when the playwright understands his trade, and realizes the gulf which yawns between the novel and the drama, the temptation to retain this fine scene of the story, or that delicately drawn character, or the other striking episode, is often too strong to be overcome, though he knows full well that these things are alien to the real play, as it ought to be. The playwright is conscious that the play-goers may look for these unessential scenes and characters and episodes, and he yields despite his judgment. Then in the end the play becomes a mere series of magic-lantern slides to illustrate the book; the real and the essential disappear behind the accidental and incidental; and the spectator cannot see the forest for the trees. The dramatizations of Scott, of Cooper, and of Dickens, whatever their temporary popularity might be, and their immediate pecuniary success, were none of them good plays, nor were they ever wholly satisfactory to those who knew and loved the original novels. And Scott, Cooper, and Dickens are all sturdy and robust story-tellers, whose tales, one would think, might readily lend themselves to the free-hand treatment and distemper illumination of the theatre. And *Uncle Tom's Cabin* has had much the same fate on the stage: the rough-hewn dramas made out of it have succeeded by no art of their own, but because of the overwhelming interest of the novel. I know of no stage version of Mrs. Stowe's story, or of any novel of Scott, of Cooper, or of Dickens, which has either organic unity or artistic symmetry.

The finer the novel, the more delicate and delightful its workmanship, the more subtle its psychology, the greater is the difficulty in dramatizing it, and the greater the ensuing disappointment. The frequent attempts to turn into a play *Vani-*

ty Fair and the *Scarlet Letter* were all
doomed to the certainty of failure, because the development of the central
character and the leading motives, as we
see them in the pages of the novelist, are
not those by which they would best be
revealed before the footlights. A true
dramatist might treat dramatically the
chief figures of Thackeray's novel or of
Hawthorne's romance. I can conceive a
Becky Sharp play and an Arthur Dimmesdale drama—the first a comedy, with un-
derlying emotion ; and the second a tragedy, noble in its simple dignity; but neither
of these possible plays would be in any
strict sense of the word dramatized from
the novel, although the germinant suggestion was derived from Thackeray and
from Hawthorne. They would be original plays, independent in form, in treatment, and in movement; much as "All
for Her" is an original play by Messrs.
Simpson and Merivale, though it was obviously suggested by the essential ideas
of *Henry Esmond* and *A Tale of Two
Cities*, which were adroitly combined by
two accomplished playwrights feeling

themselves at liberty to develop their
theme without any sense of responsibility
to the novelists. In like manner Mr.
Boucicault's admirably effective dramas,
the "Colleen Bawn" and the "Long
Strike," are founded, one on the *Collegians*
of Gerald Griffin, and the other on Mrs.
Gaskell's *Mary Barton;* but the dramatist, while availing himself freely of the
novelist's labors, held himself equally free
to borrow from them no more than he
saw fit, and felt in nowise bound to pre-
serve in the play what did not suit him
in the story. I am told that the foundation of Lord Lytton's "Richelieu" can be
discovered in a romance by G. P. R.
James; and I have heard that a little
story by Jules Sandeau was the exciting
cause of MM. Sandeau and Augier's
"Gendre de M. Poirier," the finest comedy of our century. At all times have
playwrights been prone to take a ready-
made myth. The great Greeks did it,
using Homer as a quarry from which to
get the rough blocks of marble needed
for their heroic statues; while Shakespeare and Molière found material for

more than one piece in contemporary prose-fiction. But it would be absurd to consider any of these plays as a mere dramatization of a novel.

The difficulties and disadvantages of trying to make a play out of a popular tale, when the sequence and development of the story must be retained in the drama, are so distinctly recognized by novelists who happen also to be dramatists, that they are prone to stand aside and to leave the doubtful task to others. Dumas did not himself make a play out of his romantic tale, the *Corsican Brothers*. And in the fall of 1887 there were produced in Paris two adaptations of successful novels which had been written by accomplished dramatists, *L'Abbé Constantin*, by M. Ludovic Halévy, and *L'Affaire Clémenceau*, by M. Alexandre Dumas *fils;* and in neither case did the dramatist adapt his own story. He knew better; he knew that the good novel would not make a good play ; and while the novice rushed in where the expert feared to tread, the original author stood aside ready to take the profit, but not to run the risk.

I trust that I have not suggested that there are no novels which it is profitable or advisable to adapt to the stage. Such was not my intent, at least. What I wished to point out was that a panorama was not a play ; that to make a play out of a novel properly was a most difficult task ; and that the more widely popular the story, the less likely was the resultant piece to be valuable, because of the greater pressure to retain scenes foreign to the main theme as necessarily simplified and strengthened for the theatre.

Sometimes a story is readily set on the stage, because it was planned for the theatre before it appeared as a book. M. Georges Ohnet's " Serge Panine," for example, was first written as a play and afterwards as a novel, although the piece was not performed until after the story had achieved success. Charles Reade's *Peg Woffington* is avowedly founded on the comedy of " Masks and Faces," which Reade had written in collaboration with Tom Taylor, and of which it may seem to be a dramatization. Reade also found it easy to make an effective play out of his *Never Too Late to Mend*, because this novel was itself based on " Gold," an earlier piece of his.

Nor is this *ex-post-facto* dramatization the only possible or proper adaptation of a novel. A story of straightforward emotion may often be set on the stage to advantage, and with less alteration than is demanded by the more complex novel of character. Mr. R. L. Stevenson declares that "a good serious play must be founded on one of the passionate *cruces* of life, where duty and inclination come nobly to the grapple ; and the same is true of what I call, for that reason, the dramatic novel." Now it is this dramatic novel, handling broadly a pregnant emotion, which can most often be dramatized successfully and satisfactorily. And yet, even then, the story is perhaps best set on the stage by a playwright who has never read it. This may sound like a paradox, but I can readily explain what I mean. A well-known French piece, " Miss Multon," is obviously founded on the English novel *East Lynne*. I once asked M. Eugène Nus, one of the authors of " Miss Multon,"

how he came to adapt an English book;
and he laughingly answered that neither he nor his collaborator, M. Adolphe
Bélot, had ever read *East Lynne*. At a
pause during a rehearsal of another play
of theirs, an actress had told M. Bélot
that she had just finished a story which
would make an excellent play, and there-
upon she gave him the plot of Mrs.
Wood's novel. And the plot, the primary
suggestion, the first nucleus of situation
and character, this is all these dramatists
needed; and in most cases it is all that
the dramatist ought to borrow from the
novelist. It is thus that we may account
in part for the merit of Mr. Pinero's play
" The Squire," which is perhaps more or
less remotely derived from Mr. Hardy's
Far from the Madding Crowd. Not to
have read the story he is to dramatize is,
however, a privilege possible to but few
playwrights.

The next best thing is to have the needful power to disengage the main theme
of the story and to be able to reincarnate
this in a dramatic body. A good example may be seen in " Esmeralda," the com-

2

edy which Mr. William Gillette helped Mrs. Burnett to make out of a tale of hers. But this has been done so rarely on the English-speaking stage that I must perforce seek other examples in France. As it happens I can name three plays, all founded on novels, all adapted to the stage by the novelist himself, and all really superior to the novels from which they were taken. M. Jules Sandeau's *Mademoiselle de la Seiglière* is a pretty tale, but the comedy which the late eminent comedian, M. Regnier, of the Comédie-Française, aided M. Sandeau to found upon it is far finer as a work of literature. *Le Marquis de Villemer* of George Sand is a lovely novel, but it lacks the firmness, the force, and the symmetry to be found in the play which M. Alexandre Dumas *fils* helped her to construct from it, and which, therefore, won the popular favor denied to most of her other dramatic attempts. And in like manner M. Dumas himself recomposed his *Dame aux Camélias*, and made a moving novel into one of the most moving plays of our time. In all three cases the drama is widely dif-

ferent from the story, and the many needful modifications have been made with
marvellous technical skill. Hardly any
more profitable investigation could be
suggested to the 'prentice playwright than
first to read one of these novels, and then
to compare it faithfully with the play
which its author evolved from it ; and the
student of the physics of play-making
could have no better laboratory work than
to think out the reasons for every change.

Such a student will discover, for instance, that the dramatist cannot avail
himself of one of the most effective devices of the novelist, who may keep a secret from his readers, which is either revealed to them unexpectedly and all at
once, or which they are allowed to solve
for themselves from chance hints skilfully
let fall in the course of the narrative.
But the dramatist knows that to keep a
secret from the spectator for the sake of
a single, sudden surprise is to sacrifice to
one little and temporary shock of discovery the cumulative force of a heroic
struggle against a foreseen catastrophe.
To take an example from one of the most

accomplished of Greek playwrights, the strife against awakening doubt, the wrestling with a growing conviction, the agony of final knowledge which we see in " Œdipus," and the indisputable effect these have on us, are the result of not keeping a secret. The great play of Sophocles has the interest of expectation, though every spectator might foresee and foretell the outcome of the opening situations. True dramatic interest is aroused, not by deceiving or disappointing the audience as to the end to be reached, or even by keeping it unduly in doubt as to this, but by choosing the least commonplace and most effective means of reaching that end. And true dramatic interest is sustained, not by a vulgar surprise, but by exciting the sympathy of the spectator for the character immeshed in dangers which the audience comprehend clearly—by exciting the sympathy of the spectator so that he becomes the accomplice of the playwright, putting himself in the place of the persons of the play, and feeling with them as the dread catastrophe draws nigh.

The novelist may play tricks with his readers, because he knows that they can take time to think if they are in doubt, and can even turn back a chapter or two to straighten out the sequence of events. But the dramatist knows that the spectators have no time for retrospection and for piecing together, and therefore he is not warranted in leaving them in the dark for a minute. And it is this total divergence of principle that so many novelists, and so many of those who attempt to dramatize novels, absolutely fail to apprehend. In her needless biography of Richard Brinsley Sheridan, Mrs. Oliphant found fault with the screen scene of the "School for Scandal" because we see Lady Teazle conceal herself. "It would, no doubt," she wrote, "have been higher art could the dramatist have deceived his audience as well as the personages of the play, and made us also parties in the surprise of the discovery." This criticism is simply a master‑stroke of dramatic incompetence, and it is astounding that any one able to read and write could consider that most marvellous specimen of dramatic construction, the screen scene of the "School for Scandal," without seeing that the whole effect of the situation, and half the force of the things said and done by the characters on the stage, would be lost if we did not know that Lady Teazle was in hiding within hearing of Joseph's impotent explanations, Charles's careless gayety, and Sir Peter's kindly thoughtfulness.

In a play there must be as little as possible of either confusion or doubt. As the French critic said, the laws of the drama are Logic and Movement—logic in the exposition and sequence of events, movement in the emotions presented. And here we come to another dissimilarity of the drama from prose-fiction—the need of more careful and elaborate structure in a play. A novel a man may make up as he goes along haphazard, but in a play the last word must be thought out before the first word is written. The plot must move forward unhesitatingly to its inevitable conclusion. There can be no wavering, no faltering, no lingering by the wayside. And every effect, every turn of the story must be prepared adroitly and unostentatiously. M. Legouvé calls the play-goer both exacting and inconsistent, in that he insists that everything which passes before him on the stage shall be at once foretold and unforeseen. The play-goer is shocked if anything drops from the clouds unexpected, yet he is bored if anything is unduly announced. The dramatist must now and again take the play-goers into his confidence by a chance word to which they pay no attention at the time, so that when the situation abruptly turns on itself, they say to themselves, " Why, of course, he warned us of that. What fools we were not to guess what was coming !" And then they are delighted.

In considering Lord Tennyson's " Queen Mary " when it first appeared, Mr. Henry James remarked that the " fine thing in a real drama is that, more than any other work of literary art, it needs a masterly structure, a process which makes a. demand upon an artist's rarest gifts." And then Mr. James compressed a chapter of criticism into a figure of speech. " The five-act drama," he said, "serious or humorous, poetic or prosaic, is like a box of fixed dimensions and inelastic material, into which a mass of precious things are to be packed away. . . . The precious things seem out of all proportion to the compass of the receptacle; but the artist has an assurance that with patience and skill a place may be made for each, and that nothing need be clipped or crimped, squeezed or damaged." It is this infinite patience and this surpassing skill that the ordinary theatrical adapter of a novel is wholly without. He does not acknowledge the duties of the dramatist, and he is hardly conscious even that a play is a work of literary art. Few of those who try to write for the stage, without having penetrated the secret of the drama, realize the indisputable necessity of the preliminary plan. They do not suspect that a play must needs be built as carefully and as elaborately as a cathedral, in which not only the broad nave and the massive towers but every airy pinnacle and every flying buttress contribute to the total effect. As the architect, who is primarily an artist, must do his work in full accord with the needs of the civil engineer who understands the mechanics of building, so the dramatist, who deals with human character and human passion, is guided in his labor by the precepts and practice of the mere play-maker, the expert who is master of the mechanics of the stage. The accomplished architect is his own civil engineer, and the true dramatist is a playwright also, a man fully conversant with the possibilities of the theatre and fully recognizing its limitations. "To work successfully beneath a few grave, rigid laws," said Mr. James in the criticism from which I have already quoted, "is always a strong man's highest ideal of success." This serves to explain why the sonnet with its inexorable rules has been ever a favorite with great poets, and why the drama with its metes and bounds has always had a fascination for the literary artist.

Some of the limitations of the drama are inherent in the form itself, and are therefore immutable and permanent. Some are external, and are therefore temporary and variable. For example, it has always seemed to me that inadequate attention has been given to the influence exerted on dramatic literature by the size of the theatre and by the circumstances of the performance. This influence was most potent in shaping the Greek drama, the Elizabethan plays of England, and the French tragedy under Louis XIV. The unadorned directness of Æschylus impresses us mightily; the same massive breadth of treatment we find also, although in a minor degree, in Sophocles and Euripides; on all three dramatists it was imposed by the physical conditions of the theatre. Their plays were to be performed out of doors, by actors speaking through a resonant mouthpiece in a huge mask, and lifted on high shoes so that they might be seen by thousands of spectators from all classes of the people. Of necessity the dramatist chose for his subject a familiar tale, and gave it the utmost simplicity of plot while he sought a gradually increasing intensity of emotion. The movement of his story must needs be slow; there was no change of

scene, and there was no violence of action. Thus it happens that the impassi-
ble dignity of the Greek drama was due,
not wholly to the æsthetic principles of
Greek art, but to the physical conditions
of the Greek theatre. The so-called rule
of the three unities — the rule that a
play should show but *one* action in *one*
place and in *one* day, a rule that later
critics deduced from the practice of the
Greeks—was not consciously obeyed by
Æschylus, Sophocles, or Euripides, although the most of their plays seem to
fall within it, simply from force of circumstances.

As different as may be were the large
and splendid open-air representations of
these great Greek dramas before the as-
sembled citizens of a Greek state, and
the cramped and dingy performances of
Shakespeare's plays in the rude theatre
of Queen Elizabeth's day, when the stage
was but a small platform set up at one
end of the half-roofed court-yard of an
inn. Then there was but a handful of
spectators, standing thickly in the pit or
seated in the shallow galleries close to

the actors. The stage was unencumbered
with scenery, and author and actors felt
themselves free to fill it with movement;
and so the plays of that time abound in
murders and trials, in councils and in
battles. The audience had perforce to
imagine the background of the story, and
so the authors did not hesitate to change
the scene with careless frequency. As the
noble marble theatres of Greece imposed
on the dramatist an equal severity, so the
mean, half-timbered playhouses of Elizabethan England warranted the noisy violence and the rushing eloquence and the
fiery poesy which seem to us to-day chief
among the characteristics of the dramatic
literature of that epoch.

Crossing the Channel to France, we
find that the decorum and pseudo-dignity
of tragedy under Louis XIV. are due, in
part at least, to the court plumes and
velvet coats which the actors wore even
when personating the noblest of Romans
or the simplest of Greeks; and also to the
fact that the stage was circumscribed by
a double row of benches occupied by the
courtiers. Through the ranks of these

fine gentlemen, coming and going at their
will, and chatting together freely, the Cid
and Phèdre had to make their way to a
small central space where they might
stand stock-still to declaim. Swift mo-
tion and even vigorous gesture were impossible. The wily Racine found his
account in substituting a subtle self-an-
alytic and concentrated psychologic action for purely physical movement, a
choice consonant to his genius. On the
production of Voltaire's "Sémiramis," it
is recorded that an usher had to break
through the ring of spectators seated and
standing on the stage, with a plaintive
appeal that they would make way for the
ghost of Ninus. Under conditions like
these it is no wonder that in time French
tragedy stiffened into a parody of itself.

The physical conditions of the stage
are different in every time and in every
place; they are continually changing; but
the true dramatist makes his work conform to them, consciously or unconsciously. The poet who is not a true dramatist
seeks to model a modern drama on an
ancient—a fundamental and fatal defect.

The attempt of Voltaire to imitate Sophocles was foredoomed to failure. The endeavor of many later English poets to use the Shakespearean formula is equally futile. Mr. Stedman has shrewdly pointed out that Tennyson's "Queen Mary" differs from the work of the Elizabethan dramatist in that it is the result of a "forced effort, while the models after which it is shaped were in their day an intuitive form of expression."

This forced effort is really due to a misunderstanding of the older dramatists. If Sophocles had lived in the days of Voltaire, he would have written in accordance with the physical conditions of the French theatre of that era. If Shakespeare had lived in the days of Æschylus, he would have produced Greek plays of the most sublime simplicity. Were he alive now, we may be sure that he would not construct a piece in mimicry of the Elizabethan dramatists, as Lord Tennyson chose to do. He would use the most modern form : and, incomparable craftsman as he was, he would bend to his bidding every modern improvement—music, costume, scenery, and lighting. Were Cæsar and Napoleon men of our time, they would not now fight with the short sword or the flint-lock, but with the Winchester and the Gatling.

This, I take it, is one of the chief characteristics of the true dramatist—that he sees at once when a form is outworn, and lets the dead past bury its dead; that he utilizes all the latest devices of the stage, while recognizing frankly and fully the limitations imposed by the physical conditions of the theatre. As I have already suggested, these limitations forbid not a few of the effects permissible to the novelist. No dramatist may open his story with a solitary horseman, as was once the fashion of fiction; nor can he show the hero casually rescuing the heroine from a prairie on fire, or from a slip into the rapids of Niagara; and he finds it impossible to get rid of the villain by throwing him under the wheels of a locomotive. Not only is the utilization of the forces of nature very difficult on the stage, and extremely doubtful, but the description of nature herself is out of place; and however expert the scene-painter, he cannot hope to vie with Victor Hugo or Hawthorne in calling up before the eye the grandeur or the picturesqueness of the scene where the action of the story comes to its climax.

Time was when the drama was first, and prose-fiction limped a long way after; time was when the novelists, even the greatest of them, began as playwrights. Cervantes, Le Sage, Fielding, all studied the art of character-drawing on the boards of a theatre, although no one of their plays keeps the stage to-day, while we still read with undiminished zest the humorous record of the adventures and misadventures of Don Quixote, Gil Blas, and Tom Jones. Scott was, perhaps, the first great novelist who did not learn his trade behind the scenes. It seemed to Lowell that before Fielding "real life formed rather the scenic background than the substance, and that the characters are, after all, merely players who represent certain types rather than the living types themselves." It may be suggested that the earlier novels reflected the easy expedients and artificial manners of the theatre, much as the writers may have employed the processes of the stage. Since Fielding and Scott the novel has been expanding, until it seeks to overshadow its elder brother. The old interdependence of the drama and prose-fiction has ceased; nowadays the novel and the play are independent, each with its own aims and its own methods.

While, on the one hand, there are not lacking those who see in the modern novel but a bastard epic in low prose, so there are not wanting others, novelists and critics of literature, chiefly in France, where the principles of dramatic art are better understood than elsewhere, who are so impressed by the number and magnitude of the restrictions which bind the dramatist, that they are inclined to declare the drama itself to be an outworn form. They think that the limitations imposed on the dramatist are so rigid that first-rate literary workmen will not accept them, and that first-rate literary work cannot be hoped for. These critics are on the verge of hinting that nowadays the drama is little more than a polite amusement, just as others might call oratory now little more than the art of making after-dinner speeches. They suggest that the play is sadly primitive when compared with the perfected novel of the nineteenth century. They remark that the drama can show but a corner of life, while prose-fiction may reveal almost the whole of it. They assert boldly that the drama is no longer the form of literature best suited to the treatment of the subjects in which the thinking people of to-day are interested. They declare that the novelist may grapple resolutely with a topic of the times, though the dramatist dare not scorch his fingers with a burning question. The Goncourts, in the preface of their undramatic play, " La Patrie en Danger," announced that "the drama of to-day is not literature."

It is well to mass these criticisms together that they may be met once and for all. It is true that the taste for analysis which dominates the prose-fiction of our time has affected the drama but little ; and it is not easy to say whether or not

the formulas of the theatre can be so en-
larged, modified, and made more delicate
that the dramatist can really rival the
novelist in psychologic subtlety. Of
course, if the novel continues to develop
in one direction in accordance with a
general current of literature, and if the
drama does not develop along the same
lines, then the drama will be left behind,
and it will become a mere sport, an empty
spectacle, a toy for children, spoonmeat
for babes.

A book, however fine or peculiar, delicate or spiritual, goes in time to the hundred or the thousand congenial spirits for
whom it was intended ; it may not get to
its address at once or even in its author's
life-time ; but sooner or later its message
is delivered to all who are ready to receive
it. A play can have no such fate ; and
for it there is no redemption, if once it is
damned. It cannot live by pleasing a
few only ; to earn the right to exist, it
must please the many. And this is at
the bottom of all dislike for the dramatic
form—that it appeals to the crowd, to
the broad public, to all classes alike, rich

and poor, learned and ignorant, rough and refined. And this is to me the great merit of the drama, that it cannot be dilettante, finikin, precious, narrow. It must handle broad themes broadly. It must deal with the common facts of humanity. It is the democrat of literature. Théophile Gautier, who disliked the theatre, said that an idea never found its way on the stage until it was worn threadbare in newspapers and in novels. And he was not far out. As the drama appeals to the public at large, it must consider seriously only those subjects which the public at large can understand and are interested in. There are exceptions, no doubt, now and again, when an adroit dramatist succeeds in captivating the public with a theme still in debate. M. Sardou, for example, wrote " Daniel Rochat " ten years before Mrs. Ward wrote *Robert Elsmere*, and the Frenchman's play was acted in New York for more than a hundred nights. M. Alexandre Dumas *fils* has again and again discussed on the stage marriage and divorce and other problems that vex mankind to-day.

And in Scandinavia, Henrik Ibsen, a dramatist of exceeding technical skill and abundant ethical vigor, has brought out a series of dramas (many of them successful on the stage), of which the most important is "Ghosts," wherein he considers with awful moral force the doctrine of heredity, proving by example that the sins of the fathers are visited on the children. With instances like these in our memories, we may suggest that the literary deficiencies of the drama are not in the form, but in the inexpertness or inertness of the dramatists of the day. There are few of the corner-stone facts of human life, and there are none of the crucible-tried passions of human character, which the drama cannot discuss quite as well as the novel.

Indeed, the drama is really the noblest form of literature, because it is the most direct. It calls forth the highest of literary faculties in the highest degree—the creation of character, standing firm on its own feet, and speaking for itself. The person in a play must *be* and *do*, and the spectator must see what he is, and what he does, and why. There is no narrator standing by to act as chorus, and there needs none. If the dramatist know his trade, if he have the gift of the born playwright, if his play is well made, then there is no call for explanation or analysis, no necessity of dissecting or refining, no demand for comment or sermon, no desire that any one palliate or denounce what all have seen. Actions speak louder than words. That this direct dramatic method is fine enough for the most abstruse intellectual self-questioning when the subject calls for this, and that in the mighty hand of genius it is capable of throwing light in the darkest corners and crannies of the tortured and tortuous human soul, ought not to be denied by any one who may have seen on the stage the " Œdipus " of Sophocles, the " Hamlet " of Shakspere, the " Misanthrope " of Molière, or the " Faust " of Goethe.

1889.

THE DRAMATIC OUTLOOK IN AMERICA

THE "decline of the drama" is a phrase frequently used and rarely defined. It is a vague term, and many a man who employs it would not find it easy to declare its exact meaning. More often than not the critic of the acted drama is a constant praiser of the past, which he did not see, and a pert contemner of the present, of which he is forced to see too much. To our surprise, as we study the history of the theatre, we find that this has almost always been the case, and that the drama has almost always been in a decline, just on the verge of dying, with barely strength enough to draw its last breath. And yet it still lives, and it bids fair to survive to a ripe old age.

In seeking to find a precise definition

for the phrase "decline of the drama" we
may begin by acknowledging that it cannot indicate any diminution in the popularity of the theatre; it is within the observation of even the youngest veteran
that there is a steady increase of playhouses and play-goers. Nor does it mean
that the theatres are any less magnificent
than they were, for they have never been
more commodiously arranged or more
sumptuously decorated than they are
now. And in like manner we may say
that there has been no falling off in the
splendor of theatrical spectacle; indeed,
it is often a reproach to the modern stage
that it is prone to sacrifice acting, which
is the vital essence of theatric art, to
adornment, which is but external, superficial, and accidental. But this reproach,
again, is no new thing; and it is more than
two centuries since Dryden, in the prologue to "The Rival Ladies," character-
ized the stage of his day in a terse couplet:

"You now have habits, dances, scenes, and
    rymes,
High language often—ay, and sense some-
    times."

There are some who declare that the decline of the drama means that there is a decadence of the art of acting. A certain speciousness in this assertion there may be. Since the privileges of the patent theatres of London were abolished, and since the introduction of the starring system, no longer do we see the best actors of a country massed in one or two compact companies in the chief city. They are scattered here and there throughout the world. A great actor is not content with the local reputation which satisfied Burbage and Betterton. He is ready to put a girdle round the earth in forty weeks, playing now in London, a few days after in New York, next week in San Francisco, and a month later in Australia. But although the leading performers of the country cannot any more be seen in a single evening, there has been no falling off in the histrionic art. Never has it been finer, firmer, richer, or more varied than it is now. Never have there been performers of greater skill than there are to-day, either for tragedy, comedy, history, pastoral, scene individ-

able, or poem unlimited. It is idle to
call the bead-roll of the foremost actors
of our time; but even the youngest play-
goers have seen Booth, Mr. Jefferson, Mr.
Irving, Signor Salvini, Signora Ristori,
Herr Barnay, Madame Sarah-Bernhardt,
and M. Coquelin — a galaxy not to be
matched readily in the palmy days of
which we hear so much and know so little. There is no scarcity of the best acting to-day, and the critic who may choose
to deny this assertion reminds me of
Douglas Jerrold's definition of a Conser-
vative as a man who refuses to look at
the new moon out of respect for that ancient institution the old one.

By a process of exclusion we are thus
led to declare that the decline of the
drama can mean only that the dramatic
is no longer the leading department of
literature. From the Elizabethan period,
through the Restoration and the reign of
Queen Anne, down almost to the end of
the last century, when Goldsmith gave us
" She Stoops to Conquer," and Sheridan
brought out " The Rivals " and " The
School for Scandal "—during these two

centuries the drama was the chief form of literature in our language. It is not so now, and it has not been so for nearly a hundred years. The purpose of the present paper is to point out certain of the causes of this decadence; and then to suggest certain reasons why it may fairly be presumed that the period of this decline is at last complete, and why we may expect in the near future a revival of dramatic literature among English-speaking peoples.

Like every other art, the drama has its ups and downs, its years of famine and its years of fulness. The undulatory theory is as true of literary progress as it is of light and of sound. One of these recurring periods of depression in our dramatic literature was coincident roughly with the beginning of this century, but about the time when the drama ought to have arisen out of this slough several causes combined to keep it down. These causes were chiefly four—the development of the newspaper in England, the popularity of the Waverley Novels, the Romantic revolt in France, and the perfecting of the mechanics of play-making by Scribe. Each of these four causes may be considered briefly and in turn.

The first and the least of these was the development of the newspaper. British journalism began to exert real influence less than a hundred years ago, and the impetus of expansion did not come until early in this century. A newspaper is a slice of contemporary existence; it is a daily panorama of the life of the world, with its joys, its griefs, its slow setting forth of the inevitable, its sudden surprises, and all its infinite tragedy. It has even been suggested that Shakspere, were he alive to-day, would be a journalist and not a dramatist. I am not one of those who have rashly abandoned Shakspere to adore Bacon, but I can see Lord Verulam as the editor of the London *Times* more easily than I can see the author of "Hamlet." In no exact sense of the word is the newspaper a competitor of the play; and yet the sudden extension of journalism undoubtedly tended to decrease the public interest in the drama. The newspaper called to it not a few young men who might otherwise have written for the stage, at the same time that it supplied to others the excitement and stimulus which they had been wont to seek in the theatre.

Almost contemporaneous with the development of the newspaper was the enlargement of the novel at the hands of Sir Walter Scott. In the last century Richardson and Fielding, Smollett and Goldsmith, had laid a solid foundation for English fiction; but it was not until the author of *Waverley* built up an enduring monument by his splendid series of romances that the novel rose to be a rival of the play. Scott's instant triumph and the all-embracing popularity which followed it revealed to young men of literary aspirations that the road to fame and to fortune might lie through the publisher's shop rather than through the stage-door. It is much easier to write a novel than it is to make a play; and it is very much easier to get a novel published than it is to get a play produced; and so the tendency of the young men away from the drama was strengthened.

The expansion of journalism and the extending of fiction had a twofold effect. Both movements drew away literary aspirants who were possible producers of plays, and who became journalists or novelists. And on the other hand, from among those who would have been playgoers there was carried away a certain portion able to stay its liking for the drama with the accounts of fires and robberies, of murders and battles, which it found in the newspaper, and also a certain other portion able to satisfy its longing for the romantic and the tragic with the heart-breaking tales of the novelist.

Thus it came to pass that there was a dearth of English dramatists. Mere adapters, patchers up of other men's plays, hewers of wood and drawers of water for the daily needs of the theatre — these there were then, as there are always. But real authors, men who had studied life and who could reproduce it on the stage, had their attention turned from the theatre. It was at this time in England that the divorce was first declared between literature and the drama — a divorce as ill-advised for both parties as the separation of society and politics from which we suffer here in the United States.

For a while the absence of new pieces did not signify, and the theatres continued to act the dramas they had; they revived old comedies; they restored old tragedies; they repaired the cast-off plays of the past. John Philip Kemble was then at the head of the English stage, and he had no liking for new dramas. Charles Lamb said Kemble held that all the good plays had been written. Kemble was a great actor, and it was natural for him to think that Shakspere was none too good for his own acting. Yet it may be doubted whether too frequent revivals of Shakspere's plays are signs of a healthy condition of the stage — if it be admitted that one of the chief duties of the theatre is to reflect, as best it can, the life of to-day.

At length, despite Kemble's careful management, the stock on hand was used up, and the public tired of dramatic remnants. Then for the first time the void in the English theatre began to be filled by importation from abroad—at first from

Germany, whence came "The Stranger" and "Pizarro" and other of Kotzebue's tearful and turgid dramas. But the German supply was soon exhausted, and recourse was had to the French. Until the beginning of this century the stage of England had been self-reliant. It had borrowed a play from France now and again, but it had lent quite as much as it had taken. Few even among professed students of the stage know that in the clearing-house where international borrowings are recorded there is a balance in favor of the English as against the French up to the end of the last century. For instance, there were two adaptations of "The Rivals" acted in Paris, and three of "The School for Scandal." But early in this century the balance ceased; England began to borrow indiscriminately from France; and the fair exchange soon became open robbery.

As it happened, France was able to meet this demand. Its dramatic literature had just burst the bonds which had swathed it for more than a century. "Hernani" had sounded his trumpet, and the hollow walls of Classicism had fallen with a crash. The chill stiffness and the arid discussion of the pseudo-classic drama had been swept aside by the fiery ardor of the Romantic revolt. The tragedies of the false Classics, as bare as a demonstration in geometry, gave place to the dramas of the Romantics, as full of color, of movement, and of passion as a tiger. Hugo and Dumas and their fellows found a dead dramatic literature which was nothing but words; and in its stead they made a living drama which was chiefly action. These bold, vigorous, captivating plays, made on the model of Shakspere and of Scott in a measure, were hardy enough to stand the voyage across the Channel to the land of Scott and of Shakspere. And in due season there were few theatres in Great Britain or the United States where "Thirty Years of a Gambler's Life" and "Lucretia Borgia" and "The Tower of Nesle" did not see the light of the lamps.

While the Romantics with their feverish fervor were making over the French theatre in their own image, Eugène Scribe,

4

a workman of surpassing skill in the lower walks of the drama, was engaged in
perfecting the mechanics of play-making.
Taine has told us that the art of play-
making is as susceptible of improvement
as the art of watch-making. Scribe almost succeeded in inventing a machine-
made play—and he did found a factory
for play-making. As M. Alexandre Dumas *fils* says, the dramatic art is wholly
an art of preparation : no man ever understood better than Scribe how to pre-
pare, how to twist, and how to untie the
knot which is the heart of a play. To
the presentation of the story, to the development of the central situation, Scribe
was ready to sacrifice all suggestion of
poetry, the study of character, brilliancy
of dialogue, local color, style, and even,
if need be, grammar. His plays are plots,
and little more ; and his characters are
puppets, into which he has breathed only
enough of the breath of life to enable
them to fall easily into the situations
adroitly arranged for them. He might
lay the scene of a comedy in France or in
England or in Russia : there was no touch

of local color, no insight into national characteristics. The action of all his pieces really passed in a vague, unbounded region known to the wits of Paris as *La Scribie*—Scribia—a sort of Bohemia, which is a desert country by the sea, and in which everything happens exactly as the dramatist wishes. As Scribe's plays took place in no particular country, there was no particular reason why they should not be acted in any country. They were as appropriate to England or to Russia as to France. And so it was: Scribe's comedies and the comedies of the host of collaborators who encompassed him about were translated and transferred, altered and adapted, in every capital in Europe. Localized by the translator, they were often by him presented as original; and the habit has not altogether died out, for within the last ten years a comedy has been acted in New York which the authoress claimed as her own, but which was only an adaptation from Scribe.

The principles which Scribe discovered were turned to account by certain follow-

ers of the Romantic school, and there
arose a band of melodramatic writers skilful like Scribe, and pictorial like Hugo
and Dumas. Chief among these is M.
Dennery, the author of " Don Cesar de
Bazan," " The Sea of Ice," and " The Two
Orphans." The dramas of these playwrights were also adapted, altered, and
stolen throughout the world. As Schle-
gel used to suspect a Spanish origin for
every play with an easy and varied in-
trigue, so for a while whenever we saw a
neatly constructed drama, symmetrical
and well articulated, we were inclined to
ask what Frenchman had had a hand in
its making, unwillingly and unwittingly.

When the Romantics had made themselves masters of the French stage, and
when Scribe had elaborated his system
of dramaturgic art, then and then only
did the French play go forth finally to
conquer the world. As the scanty band
of English dramatists, thinned by the
spread of the newspaper and the growth
of the novel, surrendered the control of
the English stage, the French were ready
to take it, and for fifty years they held it

with a garrison. For fifty years and more the literary quality of the plays produced in England rarely called for criticism. The best pieces of this period were the "Virginius" and "The Hunchback" of Sheridan Knowles, "The Lady of Lyons" and "Richelieu" of Lord Lytton, the "London Assurance" and "Old Heads and Young Hearts" of Dion Boucicault, and the "Masks and Faces" of Charles Reade and Tom Taylor — all effective stage-plays, no doubt, but artificial, all of them, and almost free from any vain attempt to represent contemporary society. In Emerson's words, "Life lies about us dumb; the day, as we know it, has not yet found tongue." The English stage did not try to give tongue to English thought; it was filled with impossible plays, in which Gallic emotion was mangled to fit the Procrustean bed of the British proprieties. In the process of decanting the French drama into English demijohns, the lees were shaken up and the fine flavor was lost, while an effort was made to give body to the French wine by adding British brandy. The plays known as

" Peril " and " Diplomacy " are types of
this bastard hybrid, neither French nor
English, nor anything but mulish ; and
we may say of this adapted drama what
the Western wit said of the mule, that it
has no pride of ancestry and no hope of
posterity.

The dramatic decadence in England
which began early in this century has
continued wellnigh to the present time.
Twenty-five years ago the drama in England was almost at death's door. Not
only was there an insufficiency of English plays, but the stage was treated with
contempt ; play-going was unfashionable,
and the theatre was disintegrating from
lack of leaders and for want of organiza-
tion. But now a change seems to impend.
There is a revulsion of feeling in favor of
the stage, and by this dramatic literature
will probably profit. The time seems
ripe for a renascence. Of the four causes
which long tended to prevent this at least
three are less powerful than they were
half a century ago. Journalism may still
be as attractive as ever, but prose-fiction
in England is suffering from an over-sup-

ply and from the reaction which always comes after strenuous effort. There are now no great British novelists, and the British novel is apparently entering on a period of depression not unlike that from which the drama is emerging.

At the very moment when the demand for plays is increasing, the source of supply in France is drying up. The Romantic school has been dead for years, the school of Scribe is dying, and so is the little school of melodramatists who stood midway between the other two. Rarely are the new French plays suitable for export; and the stock of old French plays is absolutely exhausted. For the fifty years in the middle of this century the French dramatists brought forth thousands of plays, emotional or amusing, intense or ingenious, melodramatic or farcical; and of all these thousands every one which had any possibility of success in English has been translated and adapted again and again. The vein is thoroughly worked out now; and although a persistent prospector may chance on a pocket, it will be but a happy accident.

The old French plays are used up, and
there are fewer new French plays than
there were. The young men who are
taking to literature in France feel themselves freer in writing fiction than in
working for the stage. As I have said
before, a novel is easier to write than a
play, and it is far easier to get before the
people. Quite recently the spread of
education, with the consequent growth
of the reading public, has at last made
the French novel as profitable as the
French play. Thus it happens that there
are not as many promising young playwrights in Paris as there were ten years
ago, and not half as many, perhaps, as
there were twenty years ago. Not only
are there fewer plays produced, but those
actually acted in Paris are far less likely
to please the American people. For one
thing, the French dramatists of to-day are
conscious of the realistic movement which
dominates the fiction of France, of Russia, and of America. The younger playwrights especially are aware of the increasing public appreciation of the more exact
presentation of the facts of life. Now the

more accurately a play conforms to life
as it is in France, the less available it is
for performance in America. What most
interests the play-goer in New York is
a representation of American life; he
does not care to see a comedy turning
on the niceties and conventionalities of
merely Parisian existence. As Realism,
and its younger brother, Naturalism,
gain in power in Paris, fewer and fewer
French plays will be fit for the American
market.

The change now to be detected in the
French drama has already been dwelt
upon by French critics, although of course
they do not see its effect on the dramatic
literature of the two English - speaking
peoples. The drama of passion, such as
the Romantics wrote, and the drama of
ingenuity, such as Scribe devised—both
admirably adapted for export — are now
seldom to be seen on the French stage.
The three chief French dramatists of
this second half of the nineteenth century
are Augier, M. Dumas, and M. Sardou.
The plays of only one of these, M. Victo-
rien Sardou, a disciple of Scribe, are

brought out successfully in Great Britain
or the United States. Of all the dramas
of M. Alexandre Dumas *fils* only one, the
" Dame aux Camélias," has held the stage
in America, despite a frequent attempt
to acclimatize others. And no one of
the modern comedies of Emile Augier—
the most wholesome and honest of the
French dramatists of the day—has been
acted at any one of the leading theatres
of New York during the score of years
since I have been a constant play-goer.
Two plays of Octave Feuillet have been
profitable in America, and two only, the
" Roman d'un Jeune Homme Pauvre"
and the "Tentation," most skilfully adapted by Dion Boucicault as " Led Astray."
Many, if not most, of the French plays of
to-day, the serious dramas as well as the
comic farces, are calculated solely for the
meridian of Paris. They are so Parisian
that they are not understood even in the
French provinces. They are as local to
the Boulevard des Italiens as are Mr.
Harrigan's amusing pieces to Mulligan's
Alley. And it would be as difficult to
transplant them to New York as it would

be to make a French adaptation of "Squatter Sovereignty."

Assertions like these are perhaps surprising to not a few who have often heard that our stage still relies on France for its supply; and it may be well to adduce a few statistics. There were in 1887–8 in New York four theatres having permanent companies and giving plays worthy of serious consideration. These were Wallack's, Daly's, the Madison Square, and the Lyceum. In these four theatres during four years (1884–5–6–7) there have been acted adaptations of only eight French plays. In 1884 "Lady Clare," a British perversion of the "Maître de Forges" of M. Georges Ohnet, was the sole example of French dramatic art at these theatres. In 1885 there were acted two versions of the "Andréa" of M. Sardou; another adaptation of the "Maître de Forges;" a translation of the "Denise" of M. Dumas; and an English play called "Impulse," derived more or less remotely from a French play called "La Maison du Mari." In 1886 came "Our Society" (based on M. Pailleron's "Monde où l'on s'ennuie "), and " Love in Harness " (based on M. Valabrègue's " Amour conjugale "). In 1887 we had a second arrangement of " Denise," a version of M. Dennery's " Martyre," and " In the Fashion," which was an adaptation from Scribe. This is the complete list of the plays adapted from the French which were produced at the four leading comedy theatres of New York during these four years. And it may be added that most of those adaptations failed to interest the public, and that no one of them was a signal success—no one of them was acted for one hundred nights. I note also that at certain other of the New York playhouses where there is no permanent company, and where the entertainment is provided by strolling stars, during the same period four other French plays were produced —" Lagardère," " Mlle. de Bressier," the " Chouans," and "Three Wives for One Husband." No one of these achieved an emphatic success. It is to be recorded also that in these four years two comedies by an American author, Mr. Bronson Howard, " One of Our Girls " and the

"Henrietta," were performed each for almost a whole season.

Figures are stubborn arguments, and those I have adduced seem to me to show that the theatres of New York are no longer dependent for their plays on the theatres of Paris. At least this is the extremely satisfactory deduction which I make from the figures. I know that statistics are edged tools, and that he who produces them is playing with fire. I can do no more than set them down and then stand before them in the humble attitude of Rufus Choate at the Italian opera, when he said to his companion, "Interpret to me this libretto, lest I dilate with the wrong emotion."

What is true of New York is not untrue of London : there, as here, the play adapted from the French is giving way to the play originally written in English. How great the change is in both cities could be shown only by a comparison with the statistics of ten and fifteen years ago—a comparison for which I have no space here. One of the chief causes of this gradual disappearance of the French drama from the English-speaking stage is the recent recognition of international stage-right. By an absurd anomaly the foreign novelist could not control the printing of his story in this country, while the foreign dramatist could protect the performance of his play. This reform has been achieved in America by judicial decision, and in England by a treaty with France. It has had a double effect. First, the foreign dramatist, French or German, now insists on full payment for his work, and thus the English-speaking dramatist is no longer forced to sell his wares in unfair competition with stolen goods. Second, the foreign dramatist insists on receiving full honor for his work, and thus the English-speaking dramatist is no longer discredited by the presumption that his play is adapted from the French. Nowadays when a new French comedy or a German farce is produced in London or in New York the foreign author's name is on the play-bill, and it is also on the check for the royalty.

The reason why so many foreign plays continue to be brought out is not far to seek. It is partly because a habit often

survives long after the exciting cause has
ceased, and partly because the conduct of
a theatre is a very ticklish task, full of
perplexity and danger, which managers
try to reduce to a minimum. To produce
a new play, absolutely untried, is always
a risky piece of business, for barely one
in three makes a hit and pays a profit.
Those in charge of theatres seek to avoid
this risk, as far as may be, by buying plays
which have already approved themselves.
If the London manager can get the pick
of Paris he discounts the hazard of a new
drama by a British author which may
or may not please the public. If the
New York manager can secure a piece already successful on the British stage or
the French, he is relieved from his doubt.
This reasoning of the manager is not without weight, and there is no harm done so
long as he takes only the best foreign
plays; the American people like to "get
the best," be it a dictionary or a drama.
But national tastes differ, and there is no
certainty that the play which succeeded
in Paris or in London may not disappoint
play-goers in New York: and of this asser-

tion American managers have abundant proof every season, with a resultant increase in the demand for American plays.

That there is already evidence of improvement in the quality as well as in the quantity of the plays written in Great Britain and the United States, I do not think any competent and candid observer would deny. I should not like to be forced to maintain the thesis that even now the average British play is better than the average British novel, although I am well aware that the average of the British novel of the past few years is low enough. But the conditions are now favorable for dramatic development, and I can see signs of its coming. There is no need to count noses; but I may suggest that "Claudian" and "Clito" are symptoms of a revival of the poetic drama; I may note that in the "Lights of London" and in the "Silver King" there was the promise of a new type of melodrama, effective and affecting, sensational if you will, but natural also, and not without the ruddy drop of human blood which alone gives vitality to the work of the pen; and

I may remark that in the authors of "Sweethearts," of "Forget-me-not," and of "The Squire" there is a little band of English playwrights who have proved their possession of the power to write comedies as simple and as direct, as ingenious in construction and almost as brilliant in dialogue, as the comedies we go to see in Paris at the Gymnase and the Vaudeville. It is true that tradition tends to keep up a tone of hard glitter in the speech of English comedy; the dramatist easily remembers that he is a follower of Sheridan, and hence comes a certain forced sparkle, a factitious smartness, a profusion of cut-and-thrust epigram perilously near to rudeness. The persons of the play are prone to take the liberty Dr. Johnson allowed himself, according to Goldsmith, who, in discussing the doctor's repartee, declared that whenever Johnson's pistol missed fire he knocked you down with the butt.

The signs of improvement in dramatic art, visible enough in Great Britain, are to be detected also in the United States. The Americans are a quicker people than

the British and of a more artistic temperament. The American novelist now sur-
passes his rival across the Atlantic ; and
perhaps the American dramatist will soon
attain to a similar superiority. It is worthy of note here that the inquiry as to
the Great American Novel, which was
frequent enough years ago, when we had
few writers of fiction, is no longer heard,
now that we have novelists a plenty.
Perhaps the search for the equally myth-
ical Great American Play will be abandoned in like manner when we have as
many good plays as we have good novels. Already has the American dramatist followed the American novelist across
the Atlantic. Sooner or later nearly
every successful American play is reproduced in London, just as every successful British play is reproduced in New
York.

Lowell tells us that Dryden's "comedies lack everything that a comedy should
have—lightness, quickness of transition,
unexpectedness of incident, easy cleverness of dialogue, and humorous contrast
of character brought out by identity of

situation." All these requisites of comedy can be seen in American novels and
in American short - stories, and they are\
beginning to be discoverable more abun-
dantly in American plays. The tendency
of our novelists has been towards subtlety, delicacy, and finish, while the tendency
of our playwrights has hitherto been far
too much in the direction of rude farce
and crude melodrama. American comedy when decorous was likely to be dull. It
is barely twenty-five years since *Vanity
Fair*, one of the earliest and sharpest of
American comic papers, had a sketch of a
dramatic critic ordering a second cup of
coffee, and saying, " Make it strong, for
I'm going to see an American comedy to-
night, and I must keep awake somehow."
I do not think that nowadays the dramatic critic finds an American comedy a
soporific ; and I know that the next morning the American dramatist is apt to
think the critic very wide-awake indeed.

Two of the chief qualifications of the
dramatist—invention and ingenuity—are
recognized characteristics of our nation.
A sense of humor is another quality not

to be denied to us; and our humor is negative as well as positive : it can take a joke as well as it can make one. The jest's prosperity lies with the audience quite as much as with the author. The kind of humor which the American most relishes turns on character. What we are keenest to seize in a story or on the stage is a touch of human nature. The play-goer, like the reader of a short-story in an American magazine, is quick to recognize a character which is at once new and true, and he is prone to pardon all else for its sake.

It is just a hundred years since Royall Tyler, afterwards Chief - Justice of Vermont, wrote "The Contrast," the first play by an American author which was acted by a professional company. This American comedy had in Jonathan the earliest of a long line of stage Yankees, and to the performance of this part by Wignell it owed most of its good-fortune. "The Contrast" proved the possibility of putting the life and the people, the manners and the customs, of our own country on the stage, and since then the most

enduring successes of our theatre have
been plays of American character. From
Hackett's Colonel Nimrod Wildfire and
Chanfrau's Mose to the later Rip Van
Winkle of Mr. Jefferson, the Davy Crock-
ett of Mr. Mayo, the Colonel Sellers of
Raymond, the Judge Slote of Florence,
and the Joshua Whitcomb of Mr. Thomp-
son, the American play-goer has been
prompt to appreciate the presentation
of American character, however harsh
and inadequate and inartistic might be
the dramatic framework in which it was
to be seen.

It would be impossible to deny that the
plays in which these characters appeared
were often feeble, forced, and false, shab-
by in structure and shambling in action.
Here we have the weakest point in the
American drama. The playwright has
not taken the trouble to learn his trade.
There is a grammar of the dramatic art
which must be mastered like any other
grammar. The writer of a comedy should
have so thorough a knowledge of the
conditions of the theatre and of the mechanics of play-making that when he puts

together his plot he does not need to think about the rules any more than he has to recall the laws of English grammar whenever he writes a letter. This technical knowledge should be digested and assimilated until its application is absolutely instinctive. No assumption is more foolish than that a man ignorant of the principles of play-making can write a play, and that afterwards a stage-manager or some other expert can " fix it up " so that it is fit to be acted. Of course it may happen that an inexperienced writer has an intuitive sense of theatrical requirements, and that he conforms to them unconsciously, but such a case must needs be rare. And perhaps this—if the parenthesis may be permitted — this is why no man knowing the stage, no actor and no manager, no dramatic author and no dramatic critic, has ever been led astray by the heresy that Shakspere's plays were written by Bacon or by any one but Shakspere himself. More often than not the novice is hopelessly ignorant even of the elements of the art, and does not understand the simplest necessities imposed by the physical conditions of the theatre. Not long ago I had a play sent to me to read, in one act of which the heroine, running away from home, is pursued by her sister, who follows her down the street, and into one of the last of a dozen little houses with gardens before them. Just how this long vista was to be shown on the stage the author had not considered. Nor did he remark that a change of scene was necessary when he caused the sister to follow the heroine through the garden into the little house, where a conversation began between them which it was expected that the audience should hear.

The best means of diffusing the needful knowledge of theatrical technic is collaboration, by which the inexperienced writer who thinks he has a subject for a play may secure the help of the expert who can teach him how to treat it. The biography of Lord Lytton has shown us that Macready was in reality part author of " The Lady of Lyons," and of " Richelieu ;" he was consulted at every step, and it was due chiefly to his understanding

of the stage that the plays were successful. The most promising of British and
American dramatists of our day have
gone to school to Scribe and to M. Sardou to spy out the secrets of their art.
Like watch-making, play-making is a
trade at which a man must serve his ap-
prenticeship; and nowhere may his *Wan-
derjahre* be more profitably spent than in
a tour of the Parisian workshops. Thus
may be acquired skill in construction—
and constructive skill is almost the first
requisite for the dramatist, if we accept
the assertion of M. Dumas that the dramatic art is an art of preparation.

All great dramatists have studied the
theatre before they wrote for it. Many
of them have had a close connection
with a playhouse. Shakspere and Molière
were players themselves, and managers
also, with a personal interest in the tak-
ings at the door—a fact which forced them
to keep touch of the public very carefully. Their dramas act well: that they
also read well was a secondary consideration. A play is something to be played;
and what is kindly called a "drama for

the closet" is a contradiction in terms;
it is a play intended not to be played.
If a drama have not the well-knit story
and the artful sequence of situation which
permit the characters to reveal themselves decently and in order, no meteor
flashes of poetry, no aurora borealis of
eloquence, can save it from the deep
damnation of its taking off the boards.
There is no more frequent phrase in the
mouth of a manager, in returning a manuscript play, than that it is " well written,"
or that it has "literary merit;" and no
phrases are falser. If the play is not well
made it cannot be well written, however
brilliant its dialogue. If the structure is
not sound and if the characters are not
rightly contrasted, there is no "literary
merit." Literature is not fine writing; it
resides rather in the conception of the
characters and in the concoction of the
story than in any elevation of language.
Théophile Gautier said that the skeleton
of every good play was a pantomime.
The deaf and dumb can seize the story
of "Hamlet" and enjoy it. All the Attic salt in Athens would not save the

tragedy of "Œdipus" if its situations were not as artistically arranged and as pathetically effective as those of "La Tosca," M. Sardou's latest one-part play.

That the drama is the highest form of literary endeavor will be denied by no true lover of Shakespeare and of Molière —the foremost figures of the two greatest modern literatures. The drama is not only the highest, it is also the broadest of all literary forms; it appeals to the plain people as directly as to the Brahmin caste. A playwright must please the public at large under penalty of not being allowed to please anybody. A novel may have its thousand readers a year and not slip out of men's memories. But if a play does not interest and hold and move a thousand spectators night after night it is soon withdrawn and laid on the shelf to be seen of men no more, In vain may the dramatist revolt at this restriction and envy the apparent privilege of the novelist. At bottom it is best that "those who live to please must please to live." Nothing is worse for an artist than the attempt to address only the " inner circle."

The advice which Joubert gives to all authors applies with double force to writers for the stage: "On doit, en écrivant, songer que les lettrés sont là; mais ce n'est pas à eux qu'il faut parler" (in writing we must remember that the men of culture are present, but it is not to them that we should speak). The dramatist must think of the boy in the gallery as well as of the young girls in the boxes. There is something wrong with the literature which appeals only to the few and which scorns the suffrages of the many. It is a puny play which is not broad enough or deep enough or human enough to please the great body of play-goers. Mankind at large it is, and not any academy, which bestows enduring fame. No clique or coterie can give a pass for the long journey of immortality: that can be had only by common consent, at an election, after due discussion, in which every man may say his say, the artisan as well as the artist. The history of literature teaches us nothing more forcibly than that the critics are as often wrong as the play-goers. It was the public which flocked to Corneille's " Cid " when the French Academy denounced it as incorrect and contrary to the rules of tragic poetry.

In literature, as in government, I believe in the ultimate wisdom of the majority. Of course under a democracy the people may be carried away for a while by a demagogue in politics or by a charlatan in letters, but this is for a season only : on a sober second thought they act as their own Supreme Court, and declare their own work unconstitutional. It is at once the danger and the glory of the dramatist in this country that the future of his art depends on the same condition as the future of our institutions—on the enlightened common-sense of the Amercan people.

1888.

THE PLAYERS

WITH the interesting complexity of metropolitan life there comes a specialization of the various social organizations. There are clubs nowadays in New York for each of the professions and for each of the arts. The lawyer, the engineer, the electrician, the railroad man has now a place in the great city where he can meet his fellows and talk shop, each after his kind. Clubs for the allied arts have been attempted, but with no notable success. Literature, music, painting, and acting all pull different ways, especially when journalism is added as a fifth wheel ; and the hardy vitality of The Salmagundi and of The Authors shows the decisive advantage of unity of pursuit among the members of an association. The times are ripe, therefore, for The Players — the club of the actor, of the theatrical manager, and of the dramatic author. The Players is the theatrical club as The Century was originally the artistic, but in The Players the domination of the professional element is carefully guarded in the constitution. Outsiders may be admitted freely, but a majority of the board of directors must always be chosen from the members who are actors, managers, or dramatists, the three divisions of the profession for whose use and behoof the club was formed.

Nearly three centuries ago an English actor, Edward Alleyn, bought the manor of Dulwich and built there the college which still exists; and more than two centuries ago an English actress, Eleanor Gwynn, gave the land at Chelsea on which stands the hospital erected through her influence. Not a score of years ago an American actor, Edwin Forrest, died, leaving his large professional earnings to maintain a home for those of his craft who should fall into poverty in their old age. These are all noble benefactions, but I doubt if any one of them is more useful in its way than the club founded only four years ago by an American actor, Edwin Booth, and intended by him to be in some measure a memorial of his father, Junius Brutus Booth (one of the foremost figures in the history of the American stage), while at the same time it should be the centre and home of all that is best in the American theatre of to-day.

For years Mr. Booth had desired to devote a proportion of his professional gains to an enterprise of this sort, and in the summer of 1887 the matter was thoroughly debated between him and certain of his friends, one of whom, Mr. T. B. Aldrich, made the felicitous suggestion that the proposed club should be named The Players. At midnight on the last day of 1888, The Players, then a hundred in number, found themselves in possession of as sumptuous a house as any in New York. Mr. Booth had bought a fine old-fashioned dwelling, No. 16 Gramercy Park, and this Mr. Stanford White had transformed into a club-house of delightful unconventionality and indisputable comfort, perfect in its most artistic decorations, in its luxurious furniture, in its ample equipment; and this perfect club-house Mr. Booth made over to The Players by deed of gift at the witching hour when the clangor of many bells declared the arrival of the year 1889. Thus The Players came into being full-armed for the struggle for existence, and not enfeebled by debts and deficiencies. It began as a proprietary club of a new sort, one in which the proprietor generously presented to the members a house ready for occupancy, that every man might at once feel at home in it.

Since the midnight when The Players gathered about Mr. Booth, before the broad fire with its blazing yule-log, and beneath Sully's noble portrait of Junius Brutus Booth, looking down with eyes of tenderness and subtle pity, the club has prospered. Its membership has increased rapidly until now it includes nearly every actor of reputation, almost all of the scanty band of American playwrights, and most of the theatrical managers of New York, with many from other cities. The attendance at the regular weekly suppers, when Saturday night stretches swiftly into Sunday morning, often reaches as high as sixty or seventy. The desire of the founder of the club is in course of accomplishment.

The constitution declares that "any male person over the age of twenty-one years shall be eligible to membership who is an actor, manager, dramatist, or other member of the dramatic profession, or who is engaged in literature, painting, sculpture, architecture, or music, or who is a patron or connoisseur of the arts." Those connected with the dramatic profession are the most numerous class in the club ; and they are the most frequent in attendance, especially on the midnight gatherings of Saturday, when the actor may rest, after two performances, serene in the consciousness of a clear forty hours before him. The next largest delegation is that of the authors, painters, sculptors, and architects—practitioners in the kindred arts with whom the player-folk foregather gladly ; as Mr. Story says in verse :

"Yet it seems to me
All arts are one—all branches on one tree—
All fingers, as it were, upon one hand."

6

The mere outsider admitted under an elastic definition of "a patron or connoisseur of the arts," is in a minority, although there is no need to accept Mr. Story's saying in prose, that an amateur is "a person who loves nothing," and a connoisseur "a person who knows nothing." Early in the history of The Players a tentative classification of its members into four divisions was rashly made by a scoffer: first, the Players proper—actors, managers, and dramatists; second, the artists; third, people who lived near Gramercy Park; and fourth, millionaires. Of millionaires there are perhaps a sparse dozen on the rolls of the club, but it is a rarity to see one within the doors. There are also two or three clergymen among The Players, including Bishop Potter and the Rev. Dr. Houghton, of the "Little Church Around the Corner," who may be called the chaplain-in-ordinary to the profession, and whose request for the closing of the theatres on Good Friday night has been acted upon by many of the managers.

In the ample hall is a large marble

mantelpiece, and on the bricks of the fireplace beneath it is inscribed this quota-
tion, written by the founder of the club :

Good frende for friendship's sake forbeare
To utter what is gossipt heare
In social chatt, lest, unawares,
Thy tonge offende thy fellowe plaiers.

Opening out of this hall is an inviting
reading - room, with an upper alcove for
writing - desks. It is from the steps of
this alcove that one can get the best view
of the portrait of Mr. Booth, framed over
the fireplace of the reading-room. This
picture was presented to The Players by
Mr. E. C. Benedict. It was painted by
Mr. John S. Sargent, and it is one of the
most brilliant, vigorous, and vivid portraits of the nineteenth century. It is a
full - length, and it represents Mr. Booth
standing negligently before the yule-log
of the hall, much as he stood on the night
when he gave the house to the club. His
attitude is easy, and the countenance is
lighted by the kindly smile so often seen
upon the face of the tragedian. What
most endears this picture to The Players

is that it is a portrait, not of the actor merely, but rather of Mr. Booth himself, as he is known to his fellow-members.

Between the fireplace and the window hangs Mr. J. Alden Weir's fine portrait of the late John Gilbert, the first of The Players to die after the club was opened. Below this is a portrait (by Zoffany) of David Garrick as Abel Drugger in Ben Jonson's play, now no longer acted. On the other side of the room is another picture of Garrick by Sir Joshua Reynolds, set off by a George Frederick Cooke by Sully and one of Naegle's portraits of Edmund Kean. Elsewhere in the reading-room are a portrait of E. A. Sothern by Mr. W. P. Frith, one of Thomas Apthorpe Cooper by Gilbert Stuart (presented by the actor's daughter), and one of Robert Palmer by Gainsborough.

In the great central hall hangs a heroic picture of Mr. Booth in the character of Richelieu, painted by the Hon. John Collier, and on the other side of the fireplace an excellent replica of Sir Thomas Lawrence's painting of John Philip Kemble as Hamlet. On the opposite side of

the room hang two of Sargent's pictures
—one of Mr. Joseph Jefferson in the character of Dr. Pangloss, the other of Lawrence Barrett in his every-day dress. Here
also are a portrait of Mrs. G. H. Gilbert
by Mrs. Dora Wheeler Keith, and one of
W. J. Florence as Sir Lucius O'Trigger by
Mr. Carroll Beckwith.

Between the hall and the dining-room
are huge safes to hold the relics and the
stray curiosities which are beginning to
accumulate. The treasures stored up do
not as yet rival those in the Green Vaults
of Dresden. Though one may seek here
in vain for a wheel of the chariot of Thes-
pis, for the mask of Aristophanes, for the
holograph manuscript of a missing comedy by Menander, for the buskin worn by
Roscius, and for a return check to the
theatre at Herculaneum, still there are
not a few curiosities almost as curious as
these. There is the sword Frederick
Lemaitre drew in the last act of "Ruy
Blas." There is the crooked staff whereon Charlotte Cushman leaned as Meg
Merrilies, when she foretold the fate of
Guy Mannering. There is the blond wig

which Fechter chose to wear as Hamlet, perhaps the most chattered about of all theatrical wigs; that it is, in reality, red and not at all blond is not surprising to those who have mused on the unrealities of life, as Hamlet himself was wont to do. There is a ring that once belonged to David Garrick, and a lock of hair that once belonged to Edmund Kean. There is a spring dagger, formerly the property of Edwin Forrest, the blade of which kindly retired within the hilt when the owner went through the motions of stabbing himself. There is a crucifix use'd by Signora Ristori in the character of Sor Teresa. Here also are the second, third, and fourth folios of Shakespeare's works, the first folio of Beaumont and Fletcher's, the first folio of Ben Jonson, and the first of Sir William Davenant with an autograph poem. Here are many autographs of high theatrical interest. Here, finally, are certain stately pieces of silver, among them a salver and pitcher presented in 1828 to Junius Brutus Booth, and the loving-cup presented to William Warren a few years before he died.

Here and there throughout the house are to be seen Shaksperian mottoes, even in the most unexpected places. That which adorns one of the mantelpieces in the grill-room is, " Mouth it, as many of our Players do." It is into this grill-room that the passage opens which the safes with the relics guard on either hand. The grill-room extends the full width of the house, and it has a broad piazza whereon the tables are set on pleasant summer days, that the members may lunch and dine in the open air. This grill-room, with its oaken beams overhead, its high wainscot, its branching silver candelabra skilfully adapted to the electric light, its novel chandelier of silver-mounted stag-horns, its blue tiled fireplaces at either end, its restful vista of a green garden beyond, its framed play-bills, and its many portraits, beneath which the walls are almost hidden, is the most beautiful room in the house and the most original.

It is seen to best advantage on Ladies' Day. The Players have but two annual feasts: one is Founder's Night, when the members assemble on New-year's Eve at midnight in commemoration of the opening of the club on the first day of 1889; and the other is Ladies' Day, when the wives and daughters of members are made welcome; this is on the afternoon of Shakspere's birthday, the 23d of April. Then is the grill-room in its glory, with the fair greenery of spring outside, with deep red roses on every table, with the moving groups of the ladies eager for the annual inspection of the paradise from which they are barred on every other day in the year. Such a gathering of beautiful and distinguished women as is seen on Ladies' Day at The Players is a rare sight even in New York.

From the evening when the club-house opened its doors, The Players have been well bestowed. On that first New-year's Eve, though the paint was scarce dry, so delicate had been the taste and so adroit the skill of the decorator, the house had no offensive air of raw newness. It appeared to be mellow from the very beginning; and as the members for the first time entered into their own, they found a fire crackling cheerfully in many a fireplace, pictures peopling the walls, and books ready to the hand, just as though the club had been in existence for years.

The books and a majority of the pictures are in the room which serves as library and as the chief portrait gallery. It is a long room, occupying most of the second floor. The bookcases rise to the height of a man's head, and the books are ready to the hand. From the walls above the portraits of the great actors and actresses of the past look down upon their successors of the present. It was the intent of the founder that the home of The Players should be a centre of light and a haven of rest for the active members of his profession. Here in the library, with its inviting arm-chairs, and its atmosphere of repose, one may keep the best of good company—that of the silent friends of the past which stand on the shelves on all sides rejecting no advances. It is an oasis where the most active of us may gladly loaf and invite his soul. "There were times," wrote Thoreau, recalling his sojourn at Walden, "when I could not afford to sacrifice the bloom of the present moment to any work, whether of the head or of the hands : I love a broad margin to my life."

In the oaken cases which stretch from one fireplace to the other is the private collection of Mr. Booth, the working library of a Shaksperian tragedian. Beyond and between the farther mantelpiece and the rear window is a major part of the theatrical collection of Lawrence Barrett; and opposite are the dramatic books of John Gilbert, a welcome gift from his widow. Other friends have filled most of the other shelves; and the gathering grows apace. Among the treasures, for example, is a collection of some thirty thousand play-bills, and over a hundred volumes of original editions of the elder dramatists, presented by Mr. Daly. In a shrine over a cabinet are half a dozen death-masks, from the unequalled collection of Mr. Laurence Hutton; and thus we may see how the author of " The School for Scandal " looked after he had departed this life, and the author of " Faust," and the author of "The Robbers." There are death - masks also of

David Garrick and of Edmund Kean, of
Marie Malibran and of Ludwig Devri-
ent, of Boucicault and of Lawrence Barrett, sad memorials of departed beauty,
genius, and power.

Above the shelves where the dust set-
tles on their biographies and on the comedies and the tragedies they acted, are
the portraits of the players of the past.
No other collection of theatrical pictures
approaches this in extent or in importance
save that of the Garrick Club in London.
As the gallery of the Garrick was begun
by the purchase of the pictures got together by Charles Mathews, so that of
The Players had its germ in the portraits
gathered by Mr. John Sleeper Clarke, a
comedian who has acted with abundant
success more than one of Mathews's characters.   To the small collection of his
brother - in - law, Mr. Booth added many
others; and since the club has opened,
and since the fact has become known that
it will gladly accept and care for portraits
of actors, not a few have been presented,
as always happens when the public is
aware that gifts of this sort are welcome.

The twoscore and more portraits in the library are all theatrical in their subjects —except that there is here a picture (supposed to be by Rembrandt Peale) of George Washington, who, under George III., was the active leader of his majesty's opposition. It was for this painting that Mr. Aldrich suggested the properly theatrical legend, "Our Leading Man."

Among these pictures there are, as all dramatic collectors will be pleased to learn, at least a dozen of the portraits painted by Naegle to be engraved for the Lopez and Wemyss series of plays—Charlotte and John Barnes, for example, Mr. and Mrs. Francis, Mr. and Mrs. Duff, Wilson, Wood, and Kean. There is also a portrait of Kean by Naegle, painted at a single sitting, so the story goes, and under peculiar circumstances. Some admirers of the actor wanted him to sit to the artist for a picture as Richard III., but he refused repeatedly. At last they invited Kean to supper after the play, and made him acquainted with Naegle, to whom he took a fancy before the feast was half over. When urged again to let the artist paint his portrait as the crookback, the actor craftily consented to pose at once, if the painter had his instruments and if he had his costume. Now these necessaries were secretly in readiness, Naegle having provided against good-fortune, and his friends having bribed Kean's dresser to be in attendance with the royal robes and plumes. So it is that Richard III. gazes down on us now a little unsteadily, as though flushed with wine rather than with victory.

It was before this portrait of Kean that Mr. Joseph Jefferson placed himself one evening when he had a night off and wished to rest. He helped himself to a biography of Kean from the shelf, and he settled himself down in an easy-chair; and there he read for two hours or more, glancing up now and again from the printed page, where the story of the wayward actor's life was told, to the painted canvas from which the man smiled back in full enjoyment of existence. Down in the grill-room there hangs a broad playbill of Drury Lane Theatre announcing that David Garrick would play Hamlet on Wednesday, February 10, 1773; and there below the name of Garrick is the name of Mr. Jefferson, who is set down to play the King. The Joseph Jefferson who now delights us as Bob Acres once pointed with pride to this play-bill, and remarked that the Joseph Jefferson who played with Garrick was his great-grand-father.

Among the other portraits in oil which fill the library and overflow out upon the staircase hall are those of Charles Mayne Young, Edwin Forrest, Mrs. Nesbit, and James Wallack by Middleton, of Henry Wallack by Inman, of E. S. Connor and R. C. Maywood by Sully, and of John Howard Payne by Wright. In the private dining-room, which is on the same floor as the library, there are half a dozen landscapes, two of them being scenes in Louisiana, painted by Mr. Jefferson. From the windows of this private dining-room may be had a grateful glimpse of the grass and the shrubbery of the shaded garden of the Tilden Library next door. "The country is lyric," said Longfellow— "the town dramatic"; and of necessity

the theatre is urban, but The Players are
fortunate in catching a breath of rusticity
from Gramercy Park in front, and from
the quiet gardens behind. In other respects, the club-house is much like other
club-houses ; it is seemly and comfortable,
restful and satisfactory. It is interesting
in itself, and for what it contains, and for
those who frequent it. It is a place to
delight all who can echo Horace Wal-
pole's assertion : " I do not love great
folks till they have pulled off their bus-
kins and put on their slippers ; because I
do not care sixpence for what they would
be thought, but for what they are."

1891

CHARLES LAMB AND THE THEATRE

AMERICANS take a peculiar delight in the humor of Charles Lamb, for he is one of the foremost of American humorists. On the roll which is headed by Benjamin Franklin, and on which the latest signatures were made by Mark Twain and Mr. Bret Harte, no name shines more brightly than Lamb's. By the captious it may be objected that he was not an American at all; but surely this should not be remembered to his discredit — it was a mere accident of birth. Elia could have taken out his naturalization papers at any time. It is related that once a worthy Scotchman, commenting on the well-known fact that all the greatest British authors had come from the far side of the Tweed, and citing in proof thereof the names of Burns and Byron and Scott, was met by the query whether Shakspere was a Scotchman also. Reluctantly enough it was acknowledged that he was not—although he had parts not unworthy of that honor. So it is with Charles Lamb. He was an Englishman; nay, more, a cockney — indeed, a cockney of the strictest sect; but he had parts not unworthy of American adoption. He had humor, high and dry, like that which England is wont to import from America in the original package. At times this humor has the same savor of irreverence towards things held sacred by commonplace humanity. Charles Lamb never hesitated to speak disrespectfully of the equator, and he was forever girding at the ordinary degrees of latitude. His jests were as smooth as they seemed reckless. He had a gift of imperturbable exaggeration; his inventive mendacity was beyond all praise; he took a proper pride in his ingenious fabrications — and these are all characteristics of the humor to be found freely along the inlets and by the hills of New England and on the prairies and in the sierras of the boundless West. He had a full sense of his high

standing as a matter-of-lie man. Moreover, he had a distaste for the straight
way and the broad road, and he had a
delight in a quiet tramp along the by-
path which pleased him personally — a
quality relished in a new country, where
a man may blaze out a track through the
woods for himself, and where academic
and even scholastic methods have hard
work to hold their own. Even his mer-
cantile training, in so far as it might be
detected, was in his favor in a land whose
merchants are princes. And behind the
mask were the features of a true man—
shrewd, keen, and quick in his judgments;
one who might make his way in the New
World as in the Old. There is something
in the man, as in the writer, which lets
him keep step to a Yankee tune. Wordsworth wrote:

> " And you must love him ere to you
> He will seem worthy of your love."

The Americans loved Lamb early, as they
did Praed and Austin Dobson — to name
two, as dissimilar as may be, of the many
British writers who have found their first

full appreciation across the Atlantic.
Charles Lamb's only acted play met in
America a far different fate from that
which befell it in England; and I have a
notion that his writings were aforetime,
and are to-day, more widely read in these
United States than in Great Britain.

"Truly was our excellent friend of the
genuine line of Yorick," said Leigh Hunt;
and although the phrase is not altogether
happy, it serves to recall two of Lamb's
chief characteristics—his humor, and his
love of the stage in general and of Shakspere in particular. That Lamb was fond
of the theatre admits of no dispute,
though he was wont to chide his mistress
freely. For Shakspere he had an affec-
tion as deep as it was broad. Whenever
these two passions crossed each other,
the theatre must needs to the wall—as in
the suggestive and paradoxical essay, "On
the Tragedies of Shakspere, considered
with Reference to their Fitness for Stage
Representation." Yet that essay yields
in charm to Elia's delightful papers: "On
Some of the Old Actors," "On the Acting of Munden," and "On the Artificial

Comedy of the Last Century." This last essay it was which Macaulay thought worth while to refute solemnly and at length. I have an idea that if Lamb could have read this posthumous refutation, he would have longed to get his hands on Macaulay's bumps to examine his phrenological development.

Lamb's humor has an Oriental extravagance to be expected in one who signed himself "Of the India House;" but his phrase had always a clerkly and clean-shaven precision not a little deceptive. In him, as in any other humorist, unusual allowance must be made for the personal equation. A humorist sees things as no one else does. He notes a tiny truth, and he likes it, and straightway he raises it to the nth, and, lo! it is a paradox. He never meant seriously that the Restoration Comedies are sound and wholesome works, as refreshing in their austere morality as the Fathers. Nor does he believe that it is a sin to set Shakspere's plays on the stage, though a simple-minded reader might think so. The light plays of Wycherley and of Farquhar did not offend Charles

Lamb, and the wit delighted him. To
him the comedies of Shakspere lost
somewhat of their range and elevation
when seen across the footlights of the
stage. A true lover of Shakspere from
his youth up, he could see more in his
mind's eye than the most lavish and
learned of stage-managers could give him.
But there are relatively few students of
Shakspere, and the mass of common
humanity had no mind's eye; it can see
only with the eye of the body, and if its
sluggish imagination is to stir at all it
must be moved by physical means. In
the theatre alone is found the sovran
magic which makes the familiar yet shad-
owy figures of Shakspere live and move
and start from the printed page into actual existence in the flesh.

Lamb's liking for the drama and for
all things pertaining to the drama was
second only to his love for Shakspere.
The ever-delightful *Tales from Shakspere*, over which he toiled despairingly
—little masterpieces which amply repaid
his travail—are scarcely more labors of
love than the *Specimens of English Dra-*

matic Poets who lived about the Time of Shakspere. To Lamb, more than to any other, is due the revival of interest in the Elizabethan dramatists. It was the fresh discovery of these old dramatic poets that gave him the impulse to write " John Woodvil." In the modern drama even the inferior contemporary farces were not despised, and some of them are re-membered now only because Lamb saw Munden act in them. Once or twice he took up the pen of the regular dramatic critic to bear witness against the play of the hour. Even then he is as gentle al-most as when he recalls the comedians of an earlier day ; he was not one of those fierce critics who, in Douglas Jerrold's phrase, review a play " as an east wind re-views an apple-tree." The acted drama, the actual stage of the present, was al-ways of interest to Lamb, and served not seldom to suggest happy illustrations for his notes on the poetic drama of the past.

It is difficult for any one who has had to read much of the writings of other theat-rical critics to speak of Charles Lamb's es-says on histrionic subjects without falling

into the extravagance of eulogy, the very
mid-summer madness of praise. There
were in his day two other lovers of the
theatre, able men both of them, having
knowledge of the stage and insight and imagination—Hazlitt and Leigh Hunt. But
what are they beside Charles Lamb? Coleridge bids us "compare Charles Lamb's
exquisite criticisms on Shakspere with
Hazlitt's round and round imitations of
them;" and to Leigh Hunt such a comparison would be still less favorable. Indeed, there is but one who has written
about the English stage at all worthy
to be set beside Charles Lamb, and he is
the author of an *Apology for the Life of
Colley Cibber*. Like Boswell, Cibber was
personally contemptible enough; and like
Boswell, he had the unknown art to make
a great book, unequalled of its kind.
There are two grand portrait galleries of
the British theatre, and it is not easy to
say which is the more artful a painter of
players—Colley Cibber or Charles Lamb.
Beside the full-length portraits of Betterton, Mrs. Barry, and Mrs. Bracegirdle—
speaking likenesses every one of them,

soundly drawn and mellow in color, as we see them in the *Apology* — may be placed the group from "Twelfth Night," which we find in the *Essays of Elia*—Mrs. Jordan as Viola, Bensley as Malvolio, Dodd as Sir Andrew, and Dickey Suett as the Clown. And Cibber, of course, was wholly without the boundless humor that has depicted for us a few of the five hundred faces of Munden, and captured on canvas a glimpse of Elliston, "joyousest of once embodied spirits."

Although only one of Lamb's dramatic pieces got itself acted at last, all of them were written for the stage. He never gave in to the heresy of the unactable drama. His plays were intended to be played, as Shakspere's were, and Marlowe's and Chapman's, and those of the other great men whom he loved and lived with. To him, as to them, a play which could not be played was no play at all. A "Drama for the Closet" is surely a patent absurdity — *bon à mettre au cabinet*, in Molière's phrase. Lamb was too keen-sighted in matters of literature not to know that form is of the essence of art, and that therefore every literary effort must conform to its purpose. He would never have accepted the latter-day theory that there are two kinds of drama—that intended to be acted, and that not intended to be acted. He was fond of paradox, no doubt; but it would be a paradox too much for even his stomach that a string of decasyllabic dialogues, lacking the relief, the color, and the movement needed by the stage, should declare itself to be a drama.

Unfortunately, the serious drama of Lamb's day was empty and inept; and so he went back for his model to the Elizabethans. He did not consider that the change in the physical conditions of the theatre forced a change in the form of the drama. The turbulent throng which stood of an afternoon in the uncovered pit of the Globe Theatre to see a boy Lady Macbeth act before a curtain declaring itself to be a royal palace, was very different from the decorous audience which sat in Drury Lane to gaze in wonder at the decorations and illuminations contrived by De Lutherbourg for the

"Christmas Tale" of David Garrick. The
stage has its changing evolutions, like
society; but Lamb, though he might con-
fess the change, did not feel it. "Hang
the age!" he cried; "I'll write for antiquity."

Now Shakspere, if he were alive,
would not write for antiquity. As a prac-
tical man, he would make skilful use of
every modern improvement. Knowing
how needful it is to catch the eye of the
public, he would turn to advantage all
later devices of scenery and stage-mech-
anism and electric-lighting. Indeed, I
doubt not that were Shakspere writing
for the stage nowadays there would not
be wanting dramatic critics to say that he
was too "sensational!" and to intimate
that he catered to the taste of the gallery.
Of a truth—if the digression may be pardoned—"Hamlet" is a very sensational
play; it has a ghost and a duel and no
end of fighting, and an indiscriminate
slaughter at the end; and before that con-
summation a young lady goes mad in
white muslin, and there is a clown at the
burying, and a fight over her grave. It

has something more and other than these physical facts; it has that within which passeth show. But it has the show-part —the mere appeal to the eye—as very few plays have. And in this quality " Macbeth " and " Romeo and Juliet " are but little inferior to " Hamlet." They could, every one of them, be acted in dumb show before a company of miners just out from the mouth of the coal-pit, and the story would be followed with interest.

This is what Théophile Gautier had in mind when he said that the skeleton of every good drama is a pantomime. Action, of course, is only the bare bones of a play, and must be covered with the living flesh of poetry. There can be no true life in a piece unless it has a solid skeleton — a play may even exist with but a scant clothing of verbiage, as we may see in any vulgar melodrama; but the finest poetry cannot give life to a drama unless the bones of its story are well knit and well jointed. This is what the Elizabethans intuitively understood, in spite of the rudeness of their stage. This is what Lamb seems never to have been able to achieve. In externals, "John Woodvil" is at times strangely like a minor work of a minor fellow - dramatist of Shakspere. We do not wonder that Godwin, happening unawares on the lines—

"To see the sun to bed and to arise,
Like some hot amorist with glowing eyes—"

came to Lamb to ask in which of the old dramatists they might be found. In internal structure, however, there is nothing Elizabethan in "John Woodvil;" there is no backbone of action—the story is invertebrate.

Lamb knew his own deficiencies in this respect, though he did not recognize their extent or their importance. He wrote to Mrs. Shelley, in 1827, while he was engaged on "The Pawnbroker's Daughter," that he could do the dialogue readily enough, "but the damned plot—I believe I must omit it altogether. The scenes come one after another like geese, not marshalled like cranes or a Hyde Park review. . . . I want some Howard Payne to sketch a skeleton of artfully-succeeding scenes through a whole play, as the courses are arranged in a cookery-book, I to find wit, passion, sentiment, character, and the like trifles; to lay in the dead colors, I'd Titianesque 'em up; to mark the channel in a cheek (smooth or furrowed, yours or mine), and where tears should course, I'd draw the water down; to say where a joke should come in, or a pun be left out; to bring my personæ on and off like a Beau Nash, and I'd Frank-·enstein them there; to bring three together on the stage at once—they are so shy with me that I can get no more than two, and there they stand until it is the time, without being the season, to withdraw them."

This is a free confession that Lamb did not know the rudiments of the playwright's trade. Bating a jot here and there for the exaggeration of the humorist, we may accept this account of his failings as fairly exact. But though he could not help himself, he could give excellent advice to his neighbor. William Godwin did not lose heart after the untimely taking off of his " Antonio," most

humorously chronicled by Lamb. He got
ready another tragedy, which Kemble declined; and he sketched out a third,
which was submitted to Lamb for sug-
gestions. In these Lamb was fertile; and
though the seed he dropped fell on stony
ground, much of it was worthy of a richer
soil. There is a letter of his wherein he
develops out of his friend's feeble plot a
strong situation, almost identical with the
second act of the "Lucrèce Borgia" of
Victor Hugo. And in a preceding letter
he had hit upon a situation very like that
on which turns the plot of the operatic
"La Favorita." These two letters of
Lamb's should be studied by all who seek
for success on the stage. They are full
not only of that criticism of life which is
the only true criticism of literature, but
of a knowledge of stage-devices, and of
the means whereby an audience may be
taken captive, very remarkable in one
who could not apply his precepts in his
own practice and for his own benefit.

Here, for instance, are a few of Lamb's
dramatic dicta: "Some such way seems
dramatic, and speaks to the eye. ... These

ocular scenes are so many great land-
marks, rememberable headlands, and
light-houses in the voyage. Macbeth's
witch has a good advice to a magic writer
what to do with his spectator :

'Show his eyes, and grieve his heart.'

You must not open any of the truth to
Dawley by means of a letter : a letter is
a feeble messenger on the stage. Some-
body, the son or his friend, must, as a
coup-de-main, be exasperated, and obliged
to tell the husband."

" I am for introducing situations, sorts
of counterparts to situations, which have
been tried in other plays—like, but not
the same. On this principle I recommended a friend like Horatio in 'The
Fair Penitent,' and on this principle I rec-
ommend a situation like Othello with relation to Desdemona's intercession to
Cassio. By-scenes may likewise receive
hints. The son may see his mother at a
mask or feast—as Romeo, Juliet. The
festivity of the company contrasts with
the strong perturbations of the individual. Dawley may be told his wife's past

unchastity at a mask by some witch-
character—as Macbeth upon the heath—
in dark sentences. This may stir his brain
and be forgot, but come in aid of stronger
proof hereafter. From this what you will
perhaps call whimsical way of counter-
parting, this honest stealing and original
mode of plagiarism, much yet, I think,
remains to be sucked.

"I am certain that you must mix up
some strong ingredients of distress to give
a savor to your pottage. Your hero
must *kill a man*, or *do something*." Earlier in the same letter Lamb had said,
"A tragic auditory wants *blood*," and had
warned Godwin not to disappoint them
of the tragic ending.

After all, there is nothing so very unusual in the fact that as a critic he knew
what ought to be done, although as a
dramatist he could not do it. Charles
Lamb was a genius, and William Godwin
was not ; but from a seat in the pit " John
Woodvil," which was never acted, is little or no better a play than " Antonio,"
which was damned.

" I am the worst hand in the world at

a plot," writes Lamb to Godwin ; and we can call " John Woodvil " to bear witness to his truth. Strictly speaking, Lamb's tragedy has no plot, although it has a story. It lacks the chain of closely link-ed incidents and situations which we are wont to demand in a play. The merits of " John Woodvil " are poetic merely, and dramatic only by accident or in in-cidentals.

A word or two here as to Lamb's poe-try may be in place. It may be doubted whether, in any strict use of the word, Lamb was a poet at all ; but as I write this the memory comes back of " Hester," and of " The Old Familiar Faces," and of certain passages in " John Woodvil," and it seems a harsh judgment. De Quincey, a kindly critic, who credited Lamb's prose with the " rarest felicity of finish and expression," called his verse " very pretty, very elegant, very tender, very beautiful," but thought that he was as one to whom the writing of verse " was a secondary and occasional function ; not his original and natural vocation — not an ἔργον, but a πάρεργον." In short, Lamb

8

had his poetic impulses and his poetic moments, but they were not long-lived. In verse, as in prose, he had always something to say; and he said it aptly, with care. His is not the polished verse that reflects only the empty image of its writer. Nor is he like that French poet of whom Malibran used to speak, and who was rich in words and poor in ideas; so the great singer described him as "trying to make a vapor-bath with a single drop of water." Lamb did not try to make a vapor-bath, and he was never reduced to a single drop of water.

Of "John Woodvil," the minor characters reveal themselves in their deeds, and they are grouped skilfully to set off the hero. But the hero himself is not a man of action—he is an elegant conversationalist. How Kemble must have longed for the fine speeches which John Woodvil pours forth! They were full of a true poetry he could well appreciate, and exactly suited to his cast of thought and histrionic habit. Yet he was right to reject the play, even had he not had "Antonio" as a warning. There is not

much to act in "Woodvil." The man
does little or nothing ; he talks and stalks,
and talks again ; once he seems about to
get drunk, which might enliven the story
somewhat, and once he fights a duel ;
but as he spares his adversary's life, even
this pleasing incident lacks finish. The
end of the drama is tame beyond endur-
ance on the stage. If, however, we put
down our opera-glasses, and read " John
Woodvil" quietly by the fireside, there
is much to reward us. The character of
Margaret is beautifully presented and developed. She is akin to Shakspere's
women both in character and in ad-
venture. Even the manly disguise she
does is a frequent Elizabethan, and indeed Shaksperian, device. The dialogue
throughout is full of the tricks of the
older dramatists, especially a constant
dropping into rhyme.

At the time Lamb wrote " John Woodvil" he was in the fresh flush of his delight in the plays of Beaumont and Fletcher, and of Marlowe. In the joy of his
discovery of these poets and of their fellows, and in the heat of the imitative fever

this gave him consciously or unconsciously, he wrote, besides the tragedy, a dramatic sketch called " The Witch." This fills a scant three pages in the collected edition of his poems, but it is an extraordinary production. It might be a fragment recovered from a lost play by the author of "The Duchess of Malfy" or " The White Devil." It has the secret, black, and midnight atmosphere. " The Witch " is as Elizabethan as " John Woodvil " in external language, and even more so in the internal feeling and thought.

Two other of Lamb's dramatic attempts may be dismissed briefly before taking the one play of his which did undergo the ordeal by fire, and was seen by the light of the lamps. One of these was " The Wife's Trial ; or the Intruding Widow," which the author declared to be a dramatic poem founded on Mr. Crabbe's tale of " The Confident." It is a story in dialogue rather than a play, although certain passages in it might not act ill. The other theatrical effort was " The Pawnbroker's Daughter," a farce in two acts. This was founded on his own essay " On

the Inconvenience of being Hanged." It
was written nearly a score of years after
"Mr. H.," and from a letter to Southey it
seems as though there was once some
hope of its being acted at the Haymarket
Theatre. " 'Tis an extravaganza," wrote
Lamb, "and like enough to follow ' Mr.
H.'" "The Pawnbroker's Daughter" is
a very whimsical piece. Like " Mr. H.,"
it was quite the equal of the average
farce of the first quarter of this century.
To us its fault is that it is not above this
average. Cutlet is an amusing character,
and so is Pendulous : in each of these are
to be seen strokes of Lamb's genuine humor. At the fall of the curtain comes
the dramatic millennium, when everybody forgives and forgets, and is happy.

The one play of Lamb's known to everybody is the two-act farce called "Mr.
H.," acted at Drury Lane Theatre, December 10, 1806, and damned out of hand.
" These are our failures," said Mr. Brum-
mel's valet ; and " Mr. H." is, in England,
always accounted one of Lamb's failures,
and quite the worst of them. It was acted
but one night. The prologue was received

with great favor, and Lamb, who was sitting with his sister in the front row of the pit, joined in the applause. The curtain fell silently at the end of the first act. During the second, some of the spectators began to hiss, and Lamb went with the crowd, "and hissed and hooted as loudly as any of his neighbors." Talfourd tells us that Elliston, who played "Mr. H.," would have tried it again, but "Lamb saw at once that the case was hopeless."

The farce has not been performed since in England, to my knowledge, save twice only. It was given at an amateur performance in 1822, by the late Charles James Mathews, when the young architect who was one day to be Elliston's legitimate successor as the airiest of light comedians, acted in this play, which had been damned at Drury Lane, and in another, which had been damned at Covent Garden—both of these misfortunes being duly set forth on the play-bill with characteristically impudent humor. And it was given once again some sixty years later at the Gaiety Theatre in London, at a single matinée, by a little band of enthusiastic young actors and actresses calling themselves "The Dramatic Students." And these are the only two appearances of "Mr. H." on the London stage.

The consensus of British criticism is that "Mr. H." was too slight for the theatre and too wire-drawn in its humor, and that its failure was what might have been expected. From this view an American, for reasons to be given hereafter, feels called upon to dissent. No doubt "Mr. H." is not one of the author's richest works; nor, on the other hand, is it as barren and bare as its critics have declared. To my mind, "Mr. H." is not at all a bad farce, as the farces of the time go : in 1806 a popular farce was not required to be as substantial and as instructive as a tragedy. It has scarcely action enough for two acts; but it is no slighter in plot and situation than the flimsy five-act comedies of Frederick Reynolds, whose "Dramatist" and "Notoriety" were very well received in their day and are carefully forgotten in ours. It is "well cut," as the French phrase it —well planned, well laid out. In the first

act is the wonder, the perplexity, the
guessing, the questioning as to the name
hidden behind this single aspirate. In
the second we have the unexpected dis-
closure, the general repulse, and the happy deliverance. The dialogue is actable;
it is fairly good stage dialogue, lending
itself to the art of the actor; and while
it is not in Lamb's best manner, it is of
far higher literary quality than can be
found in the faded afterpieces of that
time, or in the more highly colored farces
of our day. The fault of the piece, the
fatal fault, was the keeping of the secret
from the spectators. To keep a secret is
a misconception of true theatrical effect,
an improper method of sustaining dramatic suspense. An audience is interested not in what the end may be, but in
the means whereby that end is to be
reached. Before the play was done, Lamb
wrote to Manning (then in China) that
" the whole depends on the manner in
which the name is brought out." If the
audience that night had been slyly let into
the secret in an early scene, they would
have had double enjoyment in watch-

ing the futile endeavors of the *dramatis persona* to divine it, and they would not have been disappointed when Mr. Hogsflesh let slip his full patronymic. Kept in ignorance, the spectators joined the actors in speculation ; and when the word was revealed they were not amused by the disgust of the actors, so annoyed were they that they had been puzzled by a vulgar name.

Perhaps, too, there was a certain reaction after the undue expectancy raised by the prologue. Lamb wrote to Wordsworth that the number of friends they "had in the house . . . was astonishing." Now, nothing is so dangerous on the first night of a new play as a large number of the author's friends in the audience. One is greatly inclined to regret that Lamb did not yield to Elliston, and let the play be acted again. If it had had a second chance, the injudicious friends would have been absent, and the name of the hero would have been noised abroad—and once in the possession of this secret, the audience might well have laughed long and heartily at the hero's misadventures.

The reason that an American hazards
this supposition is simply that the experiment was tried in these United States,
and with success. Three months after
" Mr. H." was seen at Drury Lane it was
brought out in New York, at the Park
Theatre, where it was acted for the first
time March 16, 1807. It seems to have
made no great hit and no marked failure.
Mr. Ireland, whose *Records of the New
York Stage* is the model book of its kind
—erudite, ample, and exact—finds no record of the repetition of " Mr. H." until
1824, when it was performed " by desire."
In 1812, however, it had been produced
by the very remarkable company then
gathered at the Chestnut Street Theatre
of Philadelphia. Mr. William B. Wood,
one of the managers of the theatre, acted
Mr. H., and in the highly interesting volume of histrionic autobiography which
he published in 1854, under the title of
Personal Recollections of the Stage, he records the result in one brief and pregnant
paragraph : " Charles Lamb's excellent
farce of 'Mr. H.' met with extraordinary
success, and was played an unusual num-

ber of nights." Mr. Ireland has found
that Wood continued to act the part for
ten or a dozen years. I can hope only
doubtfully that some tidings of the better fate that befell "Mr. H." here beside
the Hudson and the Schuylkill was borne
across the Atlantic to the attic near the
Thames where Lamb received his friends
of a Wednesday evening ; but I fear me
greatly this good news did not venture
on the wintry voyage, or some record of
his pride at this unexpected reversal of
the London verdict by the higher court
of Philadelphia would linger in one of
the many letters to Manning.

"And so I go creeping on," Lamb wrote
to Manning, "since I was lamed by that
cursed fall from off the top of Drury Lane
Theatre into the pit, something more than
a year ago. However, I have been free of
the house ever since, and the house was
pretty free with me on that occasion."

It cannot be doubted that this freedom
of the theatre was a precious privilege to
one like Lamb, who had no great store of
wealth. In 1817 he moved to Russell
Street, with Drury Lane in sight from the

front window, and Covent Garden from
the back ; and here he lived for six years,
almost within sound of the orchestras of
the two patent houses, almost within hearing of the double tinkle of the bell that
rolled up the great green curtain. It was
perhaps the right of admission purchased
by " Mr. H," which gave him the chance
to study certain of the old actors about
whom Elia was to discourse in days to
come with ample humor and exact knowledge. To the end Elliston, who had acted " Mr. H.," remained a prime favorite.
To the end the playhouse was for Lamb
a haven of rest ; for there, as he looked
across the smoky flare of the footlights
into the mystic recesses beyond, he could
forget himself, and find surcease of sorrow, relief from haunting dread, and rec-
reation after "that dry drudgery at the
desk's dead wood."

The hour came when Lamb was re-
leased from doing his daily stent of labor,
but that hour took away perhaps as much
as it brought. Comrades began to drop
by the wayside ; on the stage also the
ranks of the old favorites were thinning ;

and even behind the curtain Lamb missed "the old familiar faces." The hour came when Mary Lamb, who had worked with him over the *Tales from Shakspere*, and who had sat by him in the pit at the hissing of " Mr. H.," was more and more shut out from him in the darkness of a clouded mind. The hour came when Coleridge, the friend to whom he had tied himself in youth, was taken from him. The hour came to Charles Lamb at last, as it must come to all of us, when—

"We speak of friends and their fortunes,
    And of what they did and said,
  Till the dead alone seem living,
    And the living alone seem dead.

"And at last we hardly distinguish
    Between the ghosts and the guests,
  And a mist and shadow of sadness
    Steals over our merriest jests."

1883.

TWO FRENCH THEATRICAL CRITICS

I.—M. FRANCISQUE SARCEY

TO attempt a portrait of a man of letters after the subject has already sat to two limners as accomplished as Mr. Henry James and M. Jules Lemaitre is venturesome and savors of conceit; but nearly fifteen years have passed since Mr. James made his off-hand thumbnail sketch of M. Sarcey, and M. Lemaitre's more recent and more elaborate portraiture in pastels was intended to be seen of Parisians only. Moreover, Mr. James, although he praises M. Sarcey, does so with many reserves, not to say a little grudgingly; he even echoes the opinion once current in Paris that M. Sarcey is heavy — an opinion which M. Lemaitre denounces and disproves.

It is in person that M. Sarcey is heavy
—in body, not in mind. He is portly
and thick-set, but not thick-witted. He
is short-sighted physically, but no critic
has keener insight. His judgments are
as solid and as firm-footed as his tread.
Sainte-Beuve has indicated the difference
between the "grave, learned, definitive"
criticism which penetrates and explains
and "the more alert, and more lightly
armed" criticism which gives the note to
contemporary thought. It is in the former class, among the "grave, learned, definitive" critics that M. Sarcey must be
placed ; but his serious and elaborate deci-
sions are expressed with perhaps as much
liveliness and as much point as any one
of the "more alert and more lightly
armed" may display. M. Sarcey's wit is
Voltairean in its quality, in its directness,
and in its ease. Though his arm is strong
to smite a cutting blow if need be, yet
more often than not it is with the tip of
the blade that he punctures his adversary,
fighting fairly and breaking through the
guard by skill of fence.

And of fighting M. Sarcey has had his

fill since he entered journalism more than thirty years ago. Born in 1828, he was admitted to the Normal School in 1848 in the class with Taine and Edmond About. For seven years after his graduation in 1851, he served as a professor in several small towns, constantly involved in difficulties with the officials of the Second Empire. In 1858 he gave up the desk of the teacher for that of the journalist, and coming up to Paris by the aid and advice of About, he began to write for the *Figaro*. The next year the *Opinion Nationale* was started, and M. Sarcey became its dramatic critic. In 1867 he transferred his services to the *Temps*, which is indisputably the ablest and most dignified of all Parisian newspapers; and to the *Temps*, in the number which bears the date of Monday and which appears on Sunday afternoon, M. Sarcey has contributed for now nearly a quarter of a century a weekly review of the theatres, slowly gaining in authority until for a score of years at least his primacy in Paris as a dramatic critic has been beyond question.

In addition to this hebdomadal essay
M. Sarcey has descended daily into the
thick of contemporary polemics. He
writes an article nearly every day on the
topic of the hour. When About started
the *XIXe Siècle* after the Prussian war,
M. Sarcey was his chief editorial con-
tributor, leading a lively campaign against
administrative abuses of all kinds and ex-
posing sharply the blunders of the eccle-
siastical propaganda. He has little taste
for party politics, which seem to him arid
and fruitless; but in the righting of
wrongs he is indefatigable, and in the
discussion of urban improvements, entering with ardor into all questions of water
supplies, sewerage and the like. And to
the consideration of all these problems
he brings the broad common - sense, the
stalwart logic, the robust energy which
are his chief characteristics. He has
common-sense in a most uncommon degree; and its exercise might be monoto-
nous if it were not enlivened by ironic
and playful wit.

Calling on him one day a few summers
ago and being hospitably received in the

9

spacious library which his friend M. Charles Garnier, the architect of the Opéra, has arranged for him in the wide-windowed studio of a house purchased by him from the painter who had built it for his own use, M. Sarcey told me that he was a little surprised to discover that such reputation as he might have outside of his own country was chiefly as a dramatic critic, whereas in France he was known rather as a working journalist. Sitting on the broad, square lounge below the wide window — the famous *Divan Rouge* of which M. Sarcey himself has told the legend in the pages of a French review — I suggested that perhaps this was owing to the merely local interest of the subjects the daily journalist was forced to deal with, while the Parisian dramatic critic discussed plays, many of which were likely to be exported far beyond the boundaries of France and beyond the limits of the French language. I asked him also how it was that he had never made any collection of his dramatic criticisms, or even a selection from them, as Jules Janin and Théophile Gautier had done in the past, and as Auguste Vitu of the *Figaro* and M. Jules Lemaitre of the *Débats* had more recently attempted.

I regret that I cannot recall the exact words of M. Sarcey's answer, although my recollection of the purport of his remarks is distinct enough. He said that he had not collected his weekly articles or even made a selection from them because they were journalism and not literature: the essential difference between journalism and literature being that the newspaper is meant for the moment only while the book is intended for all time, or as much of it as may be; he wrote for the *Temps* his exact opinion at the minute of the writing and having in view all the circumstances of the hour. He said that in a book an author might be moderate in assertion, but that in a newspaper, which would be thrown away between sunrise and sunset, a writer at times must needs force the note; and when it was worth while, he must be ready to declare his opinion loudly, with insistence and with undue emphasis. Of this privilege he had availed himself in the *Temps*, and this was one reason why he did not wish to see his newspaper articles revived after they had done their work. (Here I feel it proper to note that a careful reading of M. Sarcey's feuilletons every week for now nearly fourteen years has shown me that although his enthusiasm may seem at times a little overstrained, it is never factitious and it is never for an unworthy object.)

A second reason M. Sarcey gave for letting his dramatic criticisms sink into the oblivion of the back number is that he always gave his opinion frankly and fully at the instant when his impressions crystallized, and that he sometimes changed these opinions when a play was revived or when a player was seen in a new part. " Now, if I reprinted my feuilletons, "said he, laughing, " I should lose the right to contradict myself."

" To look at all sides," Lowell tells us, "and to distrust the verdict of a single mood, is, no doubt, the duty of a critic," but the hasty review of a play penned before sunrise, while the printer's boy waits for copy, is of necessity the verdict of a

single mood; and this is why M. Sarcey
feels the need of keeping his mind open
to fresh impressions, and of holding himself in readiness to modify his opinion if
good cause is shown for a reversal of the
previous decision. And the criticism to
which Lowell refers is, in one sense, literature, while the rapid reviewing of contemporary art can never be more than
journalism, tinctured always with the be-
lief that what is essential is news—first
its collection, and secondarily a comment
upon it.

In this same conversation with M. Sarcey in his library he told me that he had
planned a book on the drama—*A History of Theatrical Conventions* was to
be its exact title, I think — but that he
had done little or nothing towards it.
The drama, like every other art, is based
upon the passing of an implied agreement
between the public and the artist by which
the former allows the latter certain privileges ; and in no art are these conventions
more necessary and more obvious than in
the art of the stage. The dramatist has
but a few minutes in which to show his

action, and he can take the spectator to
but a few places ; therefore he has to se-
lect, to condense, to intensify beyond all
nature ; and the spectator has to make
allowances for the needful absence of the
fourth wall of the room in which the scene
passes, for the directness of speech, for
the omission of the non-essentials which
in real life cumber man's every movement.
Certain of these conventions are permanent, immutable, inevitable, being of the
essence of the contract, as we lawyers say,
inherent in any conceivable form of dramatic art. Certain others are accidental,
temporary, different in various countries
and in various ages.

A history of theatrical conventions as
M. Sarcey might tell it would be the story
of dramatic evolution and of the modifi-
cation of the art of the stage in accord
with the changing environment ; it would
be as vital and as pregnant and as stimu-
lating a treatise on the drama and its essential principles as one could wish. I
expressed to M. Sarcey my eagerness to
hold such a book in my hand as soon as
might be. He laughed again heartily, and

returned that he had made little progress,
and that he was in no hurry to set forth
his ideas nakedly by themselves and systematically co-ordinated. " If I once for-
mulated my theories," he said, "with
what could I fill my feuilleton — those
twelve broad columns of the *Temps* every
week ?"

What M. Sarcey has not yet done for
himself the late Becq de Fouquières attempted in a book on *L'Art de la Mise
en Scène,* the principles laid down in
which are derived mainly from M. Sarcey's essays in the *Temps.* M. de Fouquières, it is to be noted, had not M. Sarcey's knowledge, his authority, his vigor,
or his style, but his treatise is logical and
valuable, and may be recommended heartily to all American students of the stage.

That M. Sarcey should ever feel any
difficulty in filling his allotted space is in-
conceivable to those who wonder weekly
at his abundance, his variety, and his over-
flowing information. The post of dramatic critic has been held in Paris by many
distinguished men, who for the most part
regarded it with distaste and merely as a

disagreeable livelihood. Théophile Gautier was frequent in his denunciation of his theatrical servitude, speaking of himself as one toiling in the galley of journalism and chained to the oar of the feuilleton. In like manner Théodore de Banville and M. François Coppée cried aloud at their slavery, and sought every occasion for an excursus from the prescribed theatrical theme. Even M. Jules Lemaitre now and again strays from the path to discuss in the *Débats* a novel or a poem not strictly within the jurisdiction of the dramatic critic. M. Sarcey is never faint in his allegiance to the stage, and he is never short of material for examination. If there are no novelties at the theatres, there may be new books about the stage. Or if these fail there are questions of theatrical administration. Or, in default of everything else, the Comédie-Française is always open, and in the dull days of the summer it acts the older plays, the comedies and tragedies of the classical repertory, and in these M. Sarcey finds many a peg on which to hang a disquisition on dramatic esthetics. I will not say that

I have not found the same truth presented more than once in the seven hundred of M. Sarcey's weekly essays that I have read and preserved, or the same moral enforced more than once; but that is a pretty poor truth which will not bear more than one repetition.

Perhaps the first remark a regular reader of M. Sarcey's weekly review finds himself making is that the critic has a profound knowledge of the art of the stage. Of a certainty the second is to the effect that the critic very evidently delights in his work, is obviously glad to go to the theatre and pleased to express his opinion on the play and the performance. No dramatic critic was ever more conscientious than M. Sarcey, none was ever as indefatigable. Often he returns to see a piece a second time before recording his opinion in print, ready to modify his first impression and quick to note the effect produced on the real public, the broad body of average play-goers but sparsely represented on first nights.

Next to his enjoyment of his work and his conscience in the discharge of his duty, the chief characteristic of M. Sarcey is his extraordinary knowledge, his wide acquaintance with the history of the theatre in Greece, in Rome, and in France, his close hold on the thread of dramatic development, and his firm grasp of the vital principles of theatric art. He understands as no one else the theory of the drama, the why and the wherefore of every cogwheel of dramatic mechanism. He seizes the beauty of technical details, and he is fond of making this plain to the ordinary play-goer, who is conscious solely of the result and careless of the means. He has a marvellous faculty of seizing the central situation of a play and of setting this forth boldly, dwelling on the subsidiary developments of the plot only in so far as they are needful for the proper exposition of the more important point. By directing all the light on this dominating and culminating situation, the one essential and pregnant part of the piece, M. Sarcey manages to convey to the reader some notion of the effect of the acted play upon the audience—a task far above the calibre of the ordinary theatrical critics, who content themselves generally with a hap-hazard and hasty summary of the plot, bald and barren. From M. Sarcey's criticism of a play in Paris it is possible for an intelligent reader in New York to appreciate the effect of the performance and to understand the causes of its success or its failure.

His criticism—even when one is most in disagreement with his opinions—is always informed with an exact appreciation of the possibilities and the limitations of the acted drama. Here is M. Sarcey's real originality as a theatrical critic—that he criticises the acted drama as something to be acted. With the possible exception of Lessing — whom he once praised to me most cordially, declaring that he was delighted whenever he took down the *Dramaturgie* and chanced upon some dictum of the great German critic confirmatory of one of his own theories—with the exception of Lessing and of G. H. Lewes, M. Sarcey is the first dramatic critic of literary equipment who did not consider a tragedy or a comedy merely as literature and apart from its effect when acted. La Harpe and Geoffroy might have contented themselves with reading at home the plays they criticised for all the effect of the performance to be detected in their comment. Janin and Gautier were little better: to them a drama was a specimen of literature, to be judged by the rules and methods applicable to other specimens of literature.

Now no view could be more unjust to the dramatist. A play is written not to be read, primarily, but to be acted; and if it is a good play it is seen to fullest advantage only when it is acted. M. Coquelin has recently pointed out that if Shakspere and Molière, the greatest two dramatists that ever lived, were both careless as to the printing of their plays, it was perhaps because both knew that these plays were written for the theatre, and that only in the theatre could they be judged properly. Seen by the light of the lamps a play has quite another complexion from that it bears in the library. Passages pale and dull, it may be, when read coldly by the eye, are lighted by the inner fire of passion when presented in the theatre; and the solid structure of action, without which a drama is naught, may stand forth in bolder relief on the stage. A play in the hand of the reader and a play before the eye of the spectator are two very different things; and the difference between them bids fair to grow apace with the increasing attention paid nowadays to the purely pictorial side of dramatic art, to the costumes and the scenery, to the illustrative business and the ingenious management of the lights. No one knows better than M. Sarcey how sharp the difference is between the play on the stage and the play in the closet, and no one has indicated the distinction with more acumen. He judges the play before him as it impresses him and the surrounding play-goers at its performance in the theatre, and not as it might strike him on perusal alone in his study.

And this is one reason why—if it were necessary to declare the order of the critical hierarchy—I should rank M. Sarcey as a critic of the acted drama more highly than any British critic even of

the great days of British dramatic criticism, when Lamb and Hazlitt and Leigh
Hunt were practitioners of the art. The
task of Hazlitt and of Leigh Hunt was
far different from M. Sarcey's. The English drama of their day was so feeble that
few except professed students of theatrical history can now recall the names of
any play or of any playwright of that
time ; and therefore the critics devoted
themselves almost altogether to an analysis of the beauties of Shakspere and of
the art of acting as revealed by John
Philip Kemble, Sarah Siddons, and Edmund Kean. Lamb's subtle and paradoxical essays are retrospective, the best
of them, and commemorate performers
and performances held in affectionate re-
membrance. He wrote little about the
actual present, and thus he avoided the
double difficulty of dramatic criticism
as M. Sarcey has to meet it to-day in
France.

This double difficulty is, that when the
dramatic critic has to review a new play
he is called upon to do two things at
once, each incompatible with the other :

he has to judge the play, which he knows only through the medium of the acting, and he has to judge the acting, which he knows only as it is shown in the play; and thus there is a double liability to error. Neither the dramatist nor the comedian stands before the critic simply and directly—each can be seen only as the other is able and willing to declare him. It may be said that the dramatic critic does not see a new play—he sees only a performance, and this performance may be good or bad, may betray the author or reinforce him, may be fairly representative of his work and his wishes or may not. It is not the play itself that the critic sees—it is only the performance. If the play is in print, the critic may correct the impression of the single representation, or he may do so if the play be revived. Lamb and Hazlitt and Leigh Hunt, dealing almost wholly with the comedies and tragedies of the past, all of which were in print and in their possession for quiet perusal, had a far easier task than M. Sarcey's — they had to do little more than comment upon the acting or express their pre-existing opinion of the play itself. M. Sarcey has to judge both piece and the acting at the same time, and he has to judge the piece solely through the medium of the acting, and the acting solely through the medium of the piece; and it may happen that either medium refracts irregularly. Every actor, every dramatic author, every theatrical manager knows that there are "ungrateful parts" and "parts that play themselves." Out of the former the best actor can make but little, and in the latter the defects of even the poorest actor are disguised.

No dramatic critic is better aware of this double difficulty than M. Sarcey, and no one is more adroit in solving it. As far as natural gifts and an unprecedented experience can avail, he avoids the danger. He is open-minded, slow to formulate his opinion and always ready to give a play or a player a rehearing. He is never mean, never morose, never malignant. He is not one of the critics who attack a living author with the callous carelessness with which an anatomist goes to work on

a nameless cadaver. He is no more easy
to please than any other expert whose
taste is fine, though his sympathies are
broad ; but when he is pleased he is emphatic in praise. It was in the *Idle Man*,
in his wonderful panegyric of Kean's
acting, that Dana said, "I hold it to be
a low and wicked thing to keep back
from merit of any kind its due ;" and M.
Sarcey is of Dana's opinion. He is capable of dithyrambic rhapsodies of eulogy
when he is trying to warm up the Parisian
public to a proper appreciation of M.
Meilhac's "Gotte" or "Décoré," for example ; and although nobody can love
New York more than I do, sometimes one
of the *Temps* reviews of a new play at the
Vaudeville, of a revival at the Odéon,
or of a first appearance at the Français
is enough to make me homesick for
Paris.

As a critic even of the drama, M. Sarcey has his limitations. He is now and
then insular—Paris (like New York) had
its origin on an island. At times he is
dogmatic to the verge of despotism. He
has the defects of his qualities ; and the

10

first of his qualities is a robust common-
sense, which is sometimes a little commonplace and sometimes again a little
overwhelming, a little intolerant. Common-sense is an old failing of the French.
" We have almost all of us," says M. Jules
Lemaitre, "more or less Malherbe, Boileau, Voltaire, and M. Thiers in our mar-
row." A characteristic of all these typical Frenchmen was pugnacity, and this is
one of M. Sarcey's most valuable qualities.
He fights fair, but he fights hard. His
long campaign against M. Duquesnel as
the manager of the Odéon and his re-
peated attacks on the theories of the late
M. Perrin, until the death of the admin-
istrator of the Comédie - Française, are
memorable instances of M. Sarcey's te-
nacity. They are instances also of his
sagacity, for time has proved the truth of
his contentions. Again, when M. Zola
made a bitter and personal retort to a
plain-spoken criticism, M. Sarcey returned
an answer as good-tempered as any one
could wish, but as convincing and as cutting as any of M. Zola's many opponents
could desire. When M. Sarcey picks up

the gauntlet, he handles his adversary without gloves.

In the reply to M. Zola, as elsewhere, M. Sarcey confessed his abiding weakness —the incurable habit of heterophemy which makes him miscall names in almost every article he writes, setting down "Edmond" when it should be "Edward," and the like. But blunders of this sort are but trifles which any alert proof-reader might check, and which every careful reader can correct for himself. They are all of a piece with M. Sarcey's writing, which abounds in familiarities, in slang, in the technical terms of the stage, in happy-go-lucky allusions often exceedingly felicitous, and in frequent anecdotes from his wide reading or from his own experience. The result is a style of transparent ease and of indisputable sincerity. Nobody was ever in doubt as to his meaning at any time, or in doubt as to the reason why he meant what he said. To this sincerity M. Sarcey referred in his reply to M. Zola, and to it he owes, as he there declared, much of his authority as a dramatic critic. With the public, intelligence and knowledge count for much, and skill tells also, and so does wit; but nothing is as important to a critic as a reputation for integrity, for frankness, for absolute honesty in the expression of his opinions.

To keep this reputation free from suspicion M. Sarcey declined to solicit the succession of Émile Augier in the French Academy. In a dignified and pathetic letter to the public, he declared that although he believed that most of the dramatists who belonged to the Forty Immortals would vote for him, and although he believed that both before his candidacy and after his election he could criticise the plays of these dramatists as freely as he did now, yet he did not believe that the public would credit him with this fortitude. " The authority of the critic lies in the confidence of the public," he wrote; and if the public doubted whether he would speak the truth and the whole truth as frankly after he had been a candidate or after he had become an Academician, his opinion would lose half its weight. To guard his freedom he told me once he had refused all honors, even the cross of the Legion of Honor. He declared in this letter that he hesitated long, and that he knew the sacrifice he was making. If journalism had been without a representative in the Academy, perhaps he might have felt it his duty to be a candidate, but John Lemoinne was one of the Forty, and there were already two or three other journalists drawing nigh to the Academy, "who will fill most brilliantly the place I give up to them." He concluded by declaring that his ambition was to have on his tombstone the two words which would sum up his career—"Professor and Journalist."

He began as a professor, as a teacher in the schools, and now for thirty years he has been a journalist, a teacher in the newspapers, loving his work, and doing it with a conscience and a fidelity which make it an honor to the modern newspaper.

1890.

In the evolution of literature three kinds of critics have been developed. First in point of time came the critic who spoke as one having authority, who appealed to absolute standards of taste, who had no doubt as to the force of his criterions, who judged according to the strict letter of the law, and who willingly advised a poet to put his Pegasus out to grass or ordered a writer of prose to send his stalking-horse to the knacker. This critic believed in definite legislation for literature, and sometimes— when his name was Aristotle or Horace, Boileau or Pope — he codified the scattered laws, that all might obey them understandingly. Macaulay was the last English critic of this class, and even now many of his minor imitators hand down their hebdomadal judgments in the broad columns of British weeklies. In France there is to-day a man of force, acuteness, and individuality, M. Ferdinand Brunetière, who accepts this outworn creed of criticism, and who acts up to it conscientiously in the *Revue des Deux Mondes*.

The papal infallibility of the Essay on Criticism began to be doubted towards the end of the last century. Lessing, for one, had impulses of revolt against the rigidity of the rules by which literature was limited ; but the German protest of the Schlegels, for instance, was rather against the restrictions of French criticism than against a narrow method of appreciating poetry. Like the Irish clergyman who declared himself willing to " renounce the errors of the Church of Rome and to adopt those of the Church of England," most of the writers who refused to be judged by the precepts of Classicism were ready to apply with equal rigor the rules of Romanticism. But in time, out of the welter and struggle of faction came a perception of a new truth—that it is the task of the critic not to judge, but to examine, to inquire, to investigate, to see the object as it really is and to consider it with disinterested curiosity. This Sainte-Beuve attempted, though even he did not

always attain to the lofty ideal he pro-
claimed ; and to the same chilly height
Matthew Arnold tried to reach, saying
that he wished to decide nothing as of
his "own authority ; the great art of criticism is to get one's self out of the way
and to let humanity decide."

The phrase which Dr. Waldstein quoted
from Spinoza not long ago as characteristic
of the scientific mind—*Neque flere, neque
ridere, neque admirare, neque contemnere,
sed intelligere* (Neither to weep nor to
laugh, neither to admire nor to despise,
but to understand) — this may serve to
indicate the aim of scientific criticism
which judges not, which expresses no
opinions, which does not take sides, which
merely sets down, with the arid precision
of an affidavit, the facts as these are revealed by a qualitative analysis. Unfortunately, criticism as impersonal as this
is impossible ; no man can make a mere
machine of himself to register *in vacuo*.
"If there were any recognized standard
in criticism, as in apothecaries' measure,
so that, by adding a grain of praise to
this scale or taking away a scruple of

blame from that, we could make the balance manifestly even in the eyes of all men, it might be worth while to weigh Hannibal," Mr. Lowell tells us; "but when each of us stamps his own weights and warrants the impartiality of his own scales, perhaps the experiment may be wisely foregone."

The natural reaction from an impossibly callous scientific criticism which sought to suppress the personality of the critic was a criticism which was frankly individual. This is the third kind of criticism; it abdicates all inherited authority and it does not pretend to scientific exactitude. It recognizes that no standard is final, and that there is no disputing about tastes. It is aware that in the higher criticism as in the higher education there has been an abolition of the marking system, and that the critic is no longer a pedant or a pedagogue sending one author up to the head of his class and setting another in the corner with a fool's cap on his brow. It declares the honest impression of the individual at the moment of writing, not concealing the fact that even this may be different at another time. In reality Poe was a critic of this type, though he lacked frankness, and with characteristic charlatanry was prompt to appeal to the immutable standards to verify his own vagaries.

The three types of criticism have been evolved inevitably one out of the other; and the development of the third kind has not driven out the practitioners of the first and second. Critics of all three classes exist at present side by side in France, England, and America, disputing together daily in the schools. Yet the man is of more importance than the method; and a born critic can bend any theory of his art to suit his purpose. Boileau and Sainte-Beuve were both good critics, and Matthew Arnold was a good critic; and so was Lowell, who seemed rather an eclectic, not firm in following any one creed. To which theory a man gives in allegiance nowadays is mainly a question of temperament. In France, as it happens, the most brilliant critic of the younger generation, M. Jules Lemaitre,

belongs to the third class. M. Lemaitre
is a triumphant exemplar of individual
criticism, giving his opinions for what
they are worth, and presenting them so
forcibly, so picturesquely, so pleasantly,
that at least they are always worth listen-
ing to. There is no pose in his frankness,
and his apparent inconsequence is open
and honest.

In some respects M. Jules Lemaitre is
a typical Frenchman of letters. He has
the ease, the grace, the wit, the lightness
of touch, and the certainty of execution
characteristic of the best French authors.
Behind these charms he has the love of
clearness, of order, of symmetry — in a
word, of art—which is among the most
marked of French qualities. He dislikes
extravagance of any kind ; he hates harsh-
ness, violence, brutality. He inherits the
Latin tradition, and he has fed fat on the
poetry of Greece and Rome. He has
none of the liking of his contemporary,
M. Paul Bourget, for foreign countries, and
none of M. Bourget's curiosity as to foreign literature. M. Lemaitre is content
to have M. Pierre Loti do his travelling

for him, or to let Guy de Maupassant go abroad as his proxy.

M. Jules Lemaitre has not yet "come to forty years." He is still a young man. He was born in 1853, in the little village of Vennecy, on the edge of the forest of Orléans. He attended school at Orléans and then in Paris, and when he was nineteen he entered the Normal School, which of late years has given many a brilliant man to French literature. In 1875, at the age of twenty-two, he was graduated from the Normal School with high honors, and he was at once sent to the Lycée of Havre as professor of rhetoric. Here he stayed five years teaching, and yet finding time to write that first volume of verse with which most authors begin their literary career.

In 1880 he published these poems, and in the same year he was promoted and sent to Algiers. In 1883 he brought out a second book of rhymes, and he presented his double theses to the Sorbonne, whereupon he was made a doctor of letters. The thesis in French, a study of the plays of Dancourt and of the course

of French comedy after the death of Molière, was quite unconventional in its individuality, as any one may see now that
it has been published. He was again promoted, but he already thought of giving
up his professorship to venture into literature. In 1884 he asked for leave of absence and went to Paris, where he began
to contribute regularly to the *Revue
Bleue*, the most literary and the most independent of French weekly journals—
as far as may be the Parisian equivalent of the *Nation*. In a very few weeks
he made his name known to all the Parisians who care for literature. His acute
analysis of Renan was the first of his essays to attract general attention ; and
when he followed this up with equally
incisive studies of M. Zola and of M.
Georges Ohnet, he was at once accepted
as one of the most acute of contemporary French critics. As one of his biog-
raphers declares, " He was unknown in
October, 1884, and in December he was
famous." A few months later, when J. J.
Weiss resigned, M. Lemaitre was appoint-
ed dramatic critic of the *Journal des*

Débats, the position long held by Jules Janin.

His contributions to the *Revue Bleue* M. Lemaitre has four times gathered into volumes sent forth under the same title, *Les Contemporains*. Selections from his weekly articles in the *Débats* have also been collected in successive volumes called *Impressions de Théâtre*. The titles he has given to these two series of his criticisms reveal the aim of M. Lemaitre and his range. Those whom he criticises are chiefly his contemporaries, or at furthest those who have deeply and immediately influenced the men of to-day; and the criticisms themselves are chiefly his impressions. M. Lemaitre is a man of the nineteenth century, first of all, and he tells his fellow-men how the books and the plays of the nineteenth century, the authors and the actors, affect him, how they move him—in short, how they impress him at the moment regardless of any change of opinion which may come to him in the future.

Sainte-Beuve protests against those who borrow ready-made opinions, and it

must be admitted that more often than
not a ready-made opinion is a misfit.
M. Jules Lemaitre has his opinions made
to measure, and as soon as he outgrows
them they are cast aside. While he wears
them they are his own, and neither in
cut, cloth, nor style are they commonplace. He has the double qualification
of the true critic—insight and equipment.
He has humor and good-humor, and he
enjoys the play of his own wit. He is a
scholar who is often as lively and as law-
less as a schoolboy. He is at once a man
of letters and a man of the world. He
hates the smell of the lamp, and his
best work has the flavor of the good talk
that may go up the chimney when there
is a wood fire on the hearth. As he
gained experience and authority he has
become less emphatic, and he hesitates
more before coming to definite conclu-
sions. The certainty of conviction which
he brought with him from the provinces
has given way to a more Parisian scepti-
cism. His earlier criticisms were all solid-
ly constructed and stood four-square.
Renan, M. Georges Ohnet, and M. Zola

were never in any doubt as to his final opinion.

The later criticisms are more individual, more "personal"—as the French say —more impressionist, than the earlier. M. Lemaitre is quite aware that the shield is silver on one side and gold on the other, and he is no longer willing to break a lance for either metal, whichever may be nearer to him. He is open-minded, he sees both sides at once, and he sets down both the pro and the con, sometimes declining to express his own ultimate opinion, sometimes even refusing to form any opinion at all. He is fond of setting up a man of straw to act as the devil's advocate; but though this insures a full hearing of the witnesses for the defence as well as for the prosecution, it rarely prevents M. Lemaitre from getting his saint, after all, when he is resolute for the beatification. Now and again he seems indifferent, and he remains "on the fence," as we Yankees say, or rather on both sides of it at once. His attitude then is that of a lazy judge leaving the whole burden of decision on the jury. Yet he is prompt

enough, as the essays on M. Daudet's "Im-
mortel," M. Zola's "Rêve," Victor Hugo's
"Toute la Lyre," in the fourth series, show
plainly, when his opinion is clear and simple. This is evidence, were any needed,
that behind the hesitation and the apparent indifference there is a live interest in
literature, a real love for what is true, genuine, hearty, and a sharp hatred for shams.

His hatred of shams is shown in his
swift condemnation of M. Georges Ohnet's romances, perhaps unduly ferocious
in manner, although indisputably de-
served. M. Georges Ohnet is the most
popular of French novelists; his stories
sell by the hundred thousand, and he oc-
cupies the place in France which the late
E. P. Roe held in America, and which Mr.
Rider Haggard holds now in England.
There had been a general silence in the
French press about M. Ohnet's novels;
no one praised them highly, but they
pleased the public—or, at least, the half-
educated and really illiterate mass of novel readers. M. Lemaitre felt the revolt
of a scholar of refined tastes and delicate
instincts against the overpowering popu-

larity of M. Ohnet's empty triviality, and in a memorable article he "belled the cat" and he "rang the bell." Never was such an execution since Macaulay slew Montgomery. M. Lemaitre began by saying that he was in the habit of discussing literary subjects, but he hoped that he would be pardoned if he spoke now of the novels of M. Georges Ohnet; and then he went on to hold up to scorn the feeble style of M. Ohnet, the merely mechanical structure of his stories, the conventionality of his characters and their falsity to humanity, the barren absurdity of his philosophy of life and the baseness of his appeal to the prejudices of the middle class, wherein he sought for readers. In general, M. Lemaitre is keen of fence, and his weapon is the small sword of the duelling field; but to M. Ohnet he took a singlestick or a quarter-staff, and with this he beat his victim black and blue, breaking more than one bone.

Longfellow tells us that "a young critic is like a boy with a gun; he fires at every living thing he sees; he thinks only of his own skill, not of the pain he is giving."

M. Lemaitre was a young critic when he
wrote this crushing assault on M. Ohnet.
Since then he has never attempted to re-
peat the experience; it is true that there
is in France to-day no other subject as
good as M. Ohnet for a severe critic to try
his hand on. Of late when M. Lemaitre
has had to express a hostile opinion he
has been more indirect; and now he draws
blood by a dexterous insinuation adroitly
thrust under his adversary's sword arm.
Ill-disguised was his contempt for Albert
Wolff, a Parisian from Cologne, a writer of
chroniques for the *Figaro* — most perish-
able of all *articles de Paris*—one who is to
journalism what M. Georges Ohnet is to
literature. Ill-disguised is his condemnation of the part M. Henri Rochefort has
played in the French politics of the past
quarter of a century, and bitterly incisive
— corrosive almost — is the outline he
etches of the character of the man with
the immitigable grin, the man whose *Lan-
terne* helped to light the fall of the second empire, the man who has since egged
on every revolt, however bloody, however
hopeless, however foolish.

Of these adverse criticisms there are
very few indeed—a scant half-dozen, perhaps—in the threescore essays contained
in volumes of *Les Contemporains*. This
is as it should be, for he is a very narrow
critic indeed who deals more in blame
than in praise. For criticism to be profitable and pregnant, the critic must needs
dwell on the works he admires. Merely
negative criticism is sterile. The late
Edmond Scherer said that "the ideal of
criticism was to be able to praise cordially
and with enthusiasm, if need be, without
losing one's head or getting blind to defects."

Nothing is more needful for a critic
than sympathy with his subject. The
faculty of appreciation, of hearty admiration, of contagious enthusiasm even, is
among the best gifts of a true critic; and
this M. Lemaitre has in abundance. He
likes the best and the best only, but this
he likes superlatively. And he can see
the good points even of authors who do
not altogether please him; and these he is
always ready to laud in hearty fashion.

"Readers like to find themselves more

severe than the critic; and I let them have this pleasure," said Sainte - Beuve. M. Lemaitre goes far beyond his great predecessor; he delights in broad eulogy of those who appeal to his delicate sense of the exquisite in literary art. His enjoyment of " Pierre Loti," for example, of M. Daudet's *Nabab*, of Renan, is so intense that he is swept off his feet by the strong current of admiration. But though he lose his feet he keeps his head, and in his highest raptures he is never uncritical. What M. Lemaitre likes best, if not always the books best worth liking, are always at least books well worth liking; and he likes them for what is best in them, and never for their affectations, their superfluities, their contortions; and it is for these often that many a critic pretends to worship a master. M. Lemaitre's taste is keen and fine and sure; and his judgment is solid.

Although M. Lemaitre knows his classics — Greek, Latin, and French — as becomes a *Normalien*, he likes French literature better than Greek or Latin; and he likes the French literature of the nine-

teenth century better than that of the
eighteenth, or even of the seventeenth. It
is his contemporaries who most interest
him. In his clear and subtle and respectful
analysis of the characteristics of his fellow-
critic M. Ferdinand Brunetiere, M. Lemaitre confesses that while he reads Bossuet and acknowledges the power of that
most eloquent of orators, yet the reading
gives him little pleasure, "whereas often
on opening by chance a book of to-day or
of yesterday" he thrills with delight ; and
he calls on M. Brunetière to set off one
century against the other. "If, perhaps,
Corneille, Racine, Bossuet have no equiv-
alents to-day, the great century had the
equivalent of Lamartine, of Victor Hugo,
of Musset, of Michelet, of George Sand, of
Sainte-Beuve, of Flaubert, of M. Renan?
And is it my fault if I would rather read
a chapter of M. Renan than a sermon of
Bossuet, the *Nabab* than the *Princess of
Cleves*, and a certain comedy of Meilhac
and Halèvy even than a comedy of Molière?"

It is this, I think, which gives to M. Lemaitre's criticism much of its value—his

intense liking for the French literature of
to-day, and his perfect understanding of
its moods and of its methods. He has an
extraordinary dexterity in plucking out
the heart of technical mysteries. In considering a little book of sayings he took
occasion to declare the theory of maxim
making, whereby every man may be his
own La Rochefoucauld, and he supplied
an abundance of bright examples manu-
factured according to his new formulas.
In like manner he discovered the trick of
the rhythms and rhymes of Théodore de
Banville, the reviver of the rondeau and
of the ballade, and a past-master of verbal
jugglery and of acrobatic verse.

In peering into the methods of more
important literary workmen he is equally
acute. Take, for example, his study of M.
Zola — perhaps the most acute and the
most respectful analysis of M. Zola's very
remarkable powers to be found anywhere;
more elaborate than the excellent essay
written by Mr. Henry James when *Nana*
was published. M. Zola is a novelist with
a theory of his art violently promulgated
and turbulently reiterated until most peo-

ple were ready to accept his own word
for his work, and to regard his romances
as examples of the Naturalism he pro-
claimed. Now and then an adverse critic
dwelt on the inconsistencies between M.
Zola's theory and his practice, and M. Zola
himself bemoaned the occasional survivals
of the Romanticist spirit he detected in
himself. M. Lemaitre began by thrusting
this aside, and by painting M. Zola in his
true colors with a bold sweep of the brush.
" M. Zola," he declared, " is not a critic,
and he is not a Naturalistic novelist in the
meaning he himself gives to the term.
But M. Zola is an epic poet and a pessimistic poet. . . . By poet I mean a writer
who in virtue of an idea . . . notably
transforms reality, and having so transformed it gives it life." M. Lemaitre
then shows us the simple but powerful
mechanism of M. Zola's art—how he takes
a theme and sets it before the reader with
broad strokes and with typical characters
boldly differentiated and reduced almost
to their elements, but none the less alive.
Space fails here to show how M. Lemaitre
works out most convincingly the substan-

tial identity of M. Zola's massive method
with that of the epic poet, and how he
discovers in every one of M. Zola's later
fictions a Beast, a huge symbol of the
theme which that story sets forth, and a
Chorus which comments upon the events
and brings them nearer to the reader.

The essay may be recommended to all
who have a taste for criticism; I know
nothing at once more acute, more original, or truer. It may be recommended
especially to those who would like to
know what manner of writer M. Zola is,
and who yet shrink from the reading of
his novels, often drawn out and weari-
some, and nearly always foul and repul-
sive. It is M. Zola's misfortune—and it
is indubitably his own fault—that he is
judged by hearsay often, and that his books
are taken as the types of filthy fiction.
Perhaps he is more frequently condemned
than read—although sometimes the British abuse of his books has struck me as
the reaction of guilty enjoyment. Occasion serves to say in parentheses here
that while M. Zola's forcible and effective novels are painful often, while they

are dirty frequently and indefensibly, they are not immoral. It is rather in Octave Feuillet's rose-colored novels or in M. Georges Ohnet's gilt-edged fictions that we may seek insidious immorality.

M. Lemaitre indicates the misplaced dirt in M. Zola's novels, and obviously enough is himself a man of clean mind; but perhaps he lacks the inherent sternness of morality which in a man of Anglo-Saxon stock would go with an upright character like his. He has a respectful regard for the Don Juan of Molière and of Mozart, of Byron and of Musset; and he has a kindly tolerance for the disciples of Don Juan who infest French literature.

M. Lemaitre's dramatic criticisms, his *Impressions de Théâtre*, are quite as original as his more solid literary portraits, quite as fresh, quite as individual, quite as amusing. He lacks the profound knowledge of the conditions of dramatic art, the extraordinary insight into the necessary conventions upon which it is based, the thorough acquaintance with the history of the theatre in France, which have given to the foremost theatrical critic of our time, M. Francisque Sarcey, his unexampled authority. But he looks at the stage always through his own eyes, never through the opera-glass of his neighbor or the spectacles of tradition. He is fond of the theatre, and yet he readily goes outside of its walls and considers not merely the technic of the dramatist but also the ethics. Like most well-equipped and keen-witted critics, his criticism willingly broadens its vision to consider life as well as literature. Of the conventionalities and the concessions to chance which the writer of comedy avails himself freely, M. Lemaitre is tolerant, and wisely; but he is intolerant and implacable towards the false psychology and the defective ethics of the mere playwright who twists characters and misrepresents humanity to gain an effect.

The critic of the *Débats* is not content with describing the dramas of the leading theatres of Paris; he has a Thackerayan fondness for spectacles of all kinds, for the ballet, for the circus and the pantomime, for side-shows, for freaks of every degree. In all these he finds unfailing amusement and an unflagging variety of impressions. He is always alert, lively, gay ; and though he travels far afield, he is never at his wits' end. In his dramatic criticisms M. Lemaitre appears to me as a serious student of literature and of life, playing the part of a Parisian—and it is a most excellent impersonation.

Of M. Lemaitre's poems, there is no need to say anything ; they are the verses of a very clever man, no doubt, but not those of a born poet. They shine with the reflected light of his work in prose. Gray thought "even a bad verse as good a thing or better than the best observation that ever was made upon it"; but even fairly good verse is not as good a thing as the best observation that ever was made on the best verse. It is the prose and not the verse of Lessing and of Sainte-Beuve that we turn to, again and again.

Of M. Lemaitre's stories there is no need to say much : they are the tales of a very clever man, of course, but not those

of a born teller of tales. They lack a
something vague and indefinable—a flavor, a perfume, an aroma of vitality; it
is as though they were a manufacture,
rather, and not a growth. They are not
inevitable enough. They are *naïf* without being quite convincing. They have
simplicity of motive, harmony of construction, sharpness of outline, touches
of melancholy and pathos, unfailing ingenuity and wit—and yet—and yet— Of
the stories contained in the beautifully
illustrated volume called *Dix Contes* only
three or four are modern, and even
these seem to have a hint of allegory as
though there were perhaps a concealed
moral somewhere. The rest are tales of
once-upon-a-time, in Arabia, in Greece,
in Rome, as dissimilar as possible from
the *contes* of M. Daudet or of Maupassant, of M. Coppée or of M. Halévy, and
with a certain likeness to the *Contes
Philosophiques* of Voltaire. To say this
is to suggest that they are rather fables,
apologues, allegories, than short stories.

Of M. Lemaitre's play, "Revoltée,"
there is no need to say more; it is the

comedy of a very clever man indeed, but not that of a born playwright. When acted at the Odéon in 1889 it did not fail, but it did not prove a powerful attraction. When published—and to the delight of all who are fond of the drama French plays are still published as English comedies were once—it impressed the expert as likely to read better than it acted. There was abundance of wit, for example, but it was rather the wit of M. Jules Lemaitre than of his characters, and it was rather the wit of the study than of the stage. Yet "Revoltée" is an honorable attempt, and highly interesting to all who are interested in M. Lemaitre.

To sum up my opinion of these tentative endeavors in other departments of literature, M. Lemaitre is a very clever man, whose cleverness does not lead him naturally and irresistibly to poetry or to story-telling or to playwriting. What it does lead him to is criticism—criticism of literature primarily, because he loves letters, but criticism also of life at large, of man and his manners, his motives, his relation to the world and to the universe.

He has not only the faculty of straight thinking, but also that of plain speaking. He is bold and direct in his discussion of social problems, applying to their solution an unusual common-sense, and developing also an unusual understanding of the causes of apparent anomalies. I do not know anywhere a more acute statement of the relative duty of faithfulness on the part of husband and wife than is to be found in his criticism of the "Francillon" of M. Dumas *fils*. And that this statement should be found in a theatrical criticism is characteristic of M. Lemaitre's attitude; as his vision broadens and his interest in life deepens, a play or a novel is to him chiefly valuable as the theme and text of a social inquiry. Literature alone no longer satisfies.

1890.

ASIDES

I.—SHAKSPERE, MOLIÈRE, AND MODERN ENGLISH COMEDY

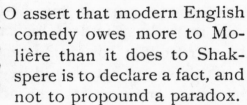O assert that modern English comedy owes more to Molière than it does to Shakspere is to declare a fact, and not to propound a paradox. The influence of Shakspere on modern English comedy, on the comic plays acted in England during the past two centuries, is indisputable, of course, but it is less in quantity and less in quality than the influence of Molière. It would be easy to go through the list of the successful English comedies acted since the death of Shakspere, and to pick out the plays, like Tobin's "Honeymoon" and Knowles's "Hunchback," written consciously in the imitation—however remote—of the Shaksperian manner. It would not be easy to

name half of the English comedies whose
form and substance had been unconsciously moulded by the example of Molière. The explanation of the seeming
paradox that the comic dramatists of
England have been more beholden to the
greatest dramatist of France than to the
greatest dramatist of England is not far
to seek. Indeed, it lies in a nutshell.
Modern English comedy is not made on
the model of Elizabethan comic drama,
and it is made—immorality apart—on the
model of the Restoration comic drama.
Now the comic dramatists of the Restoration—immorality apart—were the children of Molière. Between the Elizabethan dramatists and the dramatists of
the Restoration was a great gulf ; they
did not think alike ; they did not feel
alike ; and the larger manner of the earlier
writers was hopelessly impossible to the
younger. (Dryden is an exception ; and
Dryden is in essentials a belated Elizabethan ; at times he ventured to draw
from the nude, and some of the naked
wildness of mankind got into his work ;
but he stood alone and lonely among his

contemporaries, who had no feeling for
the nakedness of things, and whose men
and women were all clothed and in their
right mind.) The vigorous outline and
the bold stroke of the Elizabethans were
not only impossible but even repugnant
to the Restoration writers, corrupted as
they had been by the Classicism of the
French theatre. They were no longer
large-minded enough to take in the greater beauty of mighty Elizabethans. Yet
they were men of understanding and
taste, and they could appreciate to the
full the delicacy and restraint and con-
centration of the new French comedy,
which Molière had marked with his image
and superscription. Unfortunately for
themselves, when they borrowed the point
of view of the great Frenchman they forgot to borrow his sobriety and his self-
respect. They were wholly lacking in the
skill which enabled him to treat with delicacy and without offence a risky subject
—and there are few subjects more risky
than that of the "Amphitryon," for example. Where Molière glided gently and
with skilful step, his imitators trod clum-

sily and crushingly; and it is small wonder that they soon found themselves in the mire. They had a keen wit and a lively humor and a fertile invention, aided when it flagged by reminiscences of France; but they had no moral taste, no decency; and their plays have decayed rapidly for want of what would keep them sweet. But as manners and morals improved, these plays of the Restoration writers began to be thrust from the stage into the closets of librarians, until there is scarcely a single comic drama of that period holding the stage to-day. The play-goer of the fourth quarter of the nineteenth century has scant chance to see acted any comedy of Etherege, Dryden, Shadwell, Congreve, Farquhar, Wycherley, or Vanbrugh.

It is true, also, that no play of the Elizabethan period —save Shakspere's and a single piece by a single one of his contemporaries — keeps the stage. It may be that we should be as much shocked by the brutal violence of the minor Elizabethans as by the brutal indecency of the minor Restoration writers. The fact re-

mains that the play-goer of to-day can
never hope to see acted any play of Marlowe, Ford, Beaumont and Fletcher, Web-
ster, Heywood, Ben Jonson, Chapman, or
Shirley, although he may possibly by great
good-luck get a chance now and again
to see Massinger's "New Way to Pay Old
Debts." Yet the plays of some of these
authors have died hard. There is still
alive an American actress who likes to
act the "Duchess of Malfy," a tissue of
freezing horrors. There were three or
four other of the plays originally acted
under "Eliza and our James," which Macready tried vainly to warm over when
he was at the head of one of the two
great theatres of London. There were
barely a dozen of them which survived to
the end of the last century, and which
have therefore got themselves embalmed
in Mrs. Inchbald's "British Theatre" and
in the kindred collections. Among the
plays still acted at the beginning of this
century are Ben Jonson's "Alchymist"
and "Every Man in his Humor," Beaumont and Fletcher's "Rule a Wife and
have a Wife" and the "Chances," Shir-

ley's "Edward the Black Prince," and
Massinger's "City Madam," in an alteration of which, under the title of "Riches,"
Kean used to act. To-day Massinger's
"New Way to Pay Old Debts," and perhaps six out of Shakspere's twelve comedies, are all we have to represent the
comic drama of Shakspere and his contemporaries. It is true that now and
then a venturesome manager may risk a
little money in mounting one of the other
comedies of Shakspere, but the experiment never meets with popular approval,
and the revived play never lives with its
own life; it has been only galvanized
into existence; and as soon as the unnat-
ural stimulus is withdrawn it falls back
into its coffin.

Thus it appears that the Elizabethan
dramatists—with the imposing exception
of Shakspere—and the dramatists of the
Restoration have alike disappeared from
the contemporary stage. But while the
earlier drama has passed and left no sign,
the later has imposed its form on all the
dramatic writing which has followed it.
Neither the serious nor the comic work

of Shakspere and his contemporaries is a
potent influence on the drama of to-day.
More's the pity, one may say ; but the
fact is a fact, none the less. Some of the
tragic writers of the last century—Otway,
Southerne, and Rowe, for instance—reveal
plainly enough their obligation to their
great predecessors ; but popular as were
" Venice Preserved " and " Isabella " and
" Jane Shore " in their own day and for
many a long day afterwards, they are popular now no longer. The sole surviving
relics of Elizabethan imitation are Sheil's
" Evadne " and one or two of the dramas
of Sheridan Knowles ; and even in these
the imitation is little more than skin-deep.

In comedy the case is quite as plain as
in tragedy. After we have noted Sheridan Knowles's " Love Chase " and Tobin's
" Honeymoon "—which is imitated rather
from Garrick's " Katharine and Petru-
chio " than from Shakspere's own " Taming of the Shrew " — mention has been
made of all the comedies now acted which
recall even faintly the method and manner of the master. It is, indeed, a very
strange thing that the delightful comedy

of Shakspere, the wonderful woodland
wit of "As You Like It," and the rich
and rollicking humor of "Twelfth Night"
—a wit and a humor ever charged with
poetry, and as free and as fresh in this
nineteenth century as in the sixteenth
—has had little or no imitation from any
of the long line of comic dramatists who
hold their own briskly and brilliantly in
the records of English literature. But
so it is. The comedy of Shakspere has
been almost without influence on the rest
of English comedy. To find its true successor we must needs cross the Channel to France and consider carefully the
very curious likeness of certain of Musset's comedies—"On ne badine pas avec
l'amour" for example, or the "Chandelier," or the "Caprices de Marianne." It
is the comparison of a little thing with a
great, no doubt; yet is not Mr. James
right when he detects in the *quality* of
Musset's fancy something that reminds
him of Shakspere? Surely if any one is
curious to know how things have gone
on in that Bohemia which is a desert
country by the sea, he can do worse than

devote himself to the dramas of Musset, and he will find in them at least a trace of the lyric sweetness which makes all of us long to blaze our way through the forest of Arden.

The comedy of Ben Jonson, of which "Every Man in His Humor" is the consummate type, has had almost as little influence on its present successors as the more ethereal and poetic comedy of Shakspere. The comedy of "humors," of the powerful presentation of comic character and the pushing of characteristics to the very verge of caricature, made a better fight for the right to exist than any other dramatic form of the time. Even after Etherege with his "Comical Revenge; or, Love in a Tub" had set the example of a simpler and more effective development of character in emulation of the comedy of Molière—even after Etherege had been followed by Dryden and by Congreve, Vanbrugh, Wycherley, and Farquhar, not only did the comedies of Jonson continue to be acted, but later writers —like Shadwell—still imitated his exhibition of "humors." Although the school died hard, die it did at last — but for a time only. Obviously there was in it some element consonant with the national characteristics. It was not seen again in English literature until Smollett began to write novels suggested by the French "Gil Blas" (itself greatly indebted to the Spanish). Smollett's humor was both broad and elaborate, and it had a certain rough resemblance to Ben Jonson's. Smollett exerted a baleful influence on George Colman the Younger, whose very comic and very careless plays are filled with characters so sharply outlined as to be almost silhouette caricatures. Smollett's greater rival, Fielding, brought up on Molière, has been followed by Sheridan. In our century, again, the comic formulas of Ben Jonson and Smollett have been expanded by Dickens, whose influence was felt at once on the contemporary stage. Thackeray, on the other hand, traces his descent through Fielding from Molière. The two schools are irreconcilable, and between them is an irrepressible conflict. The comedy of the present day is in some measure a compromise

between the opposing schools. The form
of the better class of comedy is Molièrean,
and all of the higher and important characters are cast in the Molièrean mould,
while the lower characters, the comic
servants and scolding women, are likely
to have some survival of the "humors"
of Ben Jonson and of the kindred carica-
tural methods of his followers, Smollett
and Dickens.

The reason why the influence of Molière
is more potent on the form of English
comedy than the influence of Shakspere
is not far to seek. It is that Molière represents a later stage of the development
of play-making. In outward structure the
plays of the great French dramatists who
wrote under Louis XIV. are more symmetrical and better built than the plays
of the great English dramatists who wrote
under Elizabeth and James I. Not only
is the external form simpler and clearer,
but the internal unity is in general more
marked. It is hard to say just what is
the subject of many Elizabethan dramas;
there is never any difficulty in declaring

at once the subject of any drama, comic or tragic, by Corneille, Molière, or Racine. The English play is often rough and rugged even when it is not formless and shapeless. The French play is always smooth and sharply outlined and logically complete. The English poet gives us only too often an inchoate and incongruous mass of poetic matter, a rude lump of ore, from which we must disengage the precious metal as best we may. The French poet is not as rich and he is not as free-handed; he fuses his ore and refines his gold and beats it thin and polishes it and fashions it curiously. In looking at the English drama of the Shaksperian epoch, the prevailing impression one gets is an impression of main strength, of rude vigor, of native wildness and profusion. In looking at the French drama of the Molièrean epoch, the prevailing impression is an impression of firm and delicate art. To write in the Elizabethan manner is tolerable only in those who have the lofty stature and giant grasp of the Elizabethans. In mere mass of native ability the authors around

Shakspere were greater than the authors around Molière; and yet nowadays writers for the stage will do better if they rather avail themselves of the more orderly methods of the contemporaries of Molière. But even in France comedy was far more vigorous than tragedy; while there is a long stride from Corneille and Racine to Victor Hugo, Molière was followed by Regnard, Marivaux, Lesage, and Beaumarchais. In England the imitation of French tragic models was short-lived, while the use of the French formula of comedy, expanded to suit English tastes, continues to this day.

The cause of the abiding influence of Molière and of the fading influence of Shakspere is to be sought, I think, in the changes in the physical conditions of the stage. Molière began to write half a century after Shakspere ceased to write; and in that half-century many and marked changes had taken place in the arrangement and constitution of the theatre. Shakspere acted in a theatre bearing a very close resemblance to the court of an inn—from which, indeed, it was an evolu-

tion ; his plays were performed on a pro-
jecting platform before a turbulent throng
standing and brawling in the pit, scarcely
sheltered from the sun and rain. Molière acted in a theatre, well roofed, water-
tight, made over from a tennis-court ; and
his plays were performed before and between rows of seated courtiers, often in
the presence of the courteous king. The
stage appliances of Shakspere's time were
so few and scanty as to be almost wholly
absent. The stage-machinery which Molière could command and of which he
made use in the "Festin de Pierre" was
elaborate and differed but little from that
now available. In fact, the difference between the theatre as organized in the time
of Shakspere and the theatre as organized
in the time of Molière is enormous and
radical ; whereas the difference between
the theatre as it was organized in the
time of Molière and as it is organized to-
day is unessential and insignificant. The
physical conditions of the stage under
Shakspere are altogether other than those
of our time, while the physical conditions
of the stage under Molière are substan-

tially identical with those of our time. Therefore is it, in great measure, that the only English comedies which have survived fitly are those influenced by the art of Molière and made according to his formula and in accord with the environment of to-day.

1883.

II.—THE "OLD COMEDIES"

EVERY year or so some manager in New York or Boston announces a series of revivals of the "Old Comedies." Every now and again the theatrical critics of these cities are moved to contrast—to its disadvantage — some contemporary comic drama with these same "Old Comedies." There may be, therefore, interest in an inquiry as to these "Old Comedies," their titles, their authors, their real value, and their traditional reputation.

First of all, what are the "Old Comedies," as the term is used by the theatrical critic of the last quarter of the nineteenth century? The answer to this question is simple. They are a score or so of more or less comic plays written by various English dramatists at intervals during the hundred and fifty years intervening between 1700 and 1850, and distinguished from among the thousands of other comic dramas written during that century and a half by the fact that they have had vitality enough to keep the stage. In all departments of literature there is a struggle for existence, and the acknowledged classics are the results of the survival of the fittest. It is by the same process of natural selection that twenty or thirty "Old Comedies" have been picked out of the thousand or two which were acted contemporaneously with them. It is with these picked and proved troops that the new English or American comedy is measured; and it is from a hasty comparison of the best of the past with the average of the present that the decline of the drama is declared. The unfairness of the proceeding needs no comment. When beneficent Time has thrashed out the dramatic literature of our day it will be possible to winnow comic plays written

by men now living, which in due season
will take their place among the "Old
Comedies," and which will then hold
their own against all but the very best of
their companions. And as the best of the
comedies of our day are not unequal to
the best of the comedies of the past century and a half, so the worst of the plays
of our day are not worse than the worst
of the plays of the past. The ordinary
play-goer speaks of the plays of the past
with respect because he is ignorant about
them and takes the unknown for the magnificent. The ordinary reader lacks cour-
age to attack the immense mass of the
plays of the past. There was in the
library of the Reverend Mr. Arthur
Dimmesdale a ponderous tome which the
historian of the erring clergyman's strug-
gles deems to have been "a work of vast
ability in the somniferous school of literature." There is in the library of every
dramatic collector a series of collections
of little volumes containing some few
chosen samples of the plays of the past;
and the contents of these little volumes
are of a certainty closely akin to the con-

tents of the ponderous tome, in that they all have a powerful soporific virtue. And these little volumes contain less than one in twenty of the plays actually acted : they contain only the more readable specimens.

In 1873 or thereabouts Mr. W. S. Gilbert made an examination of the voluminous *Account of the English Stage from 1660 to 1830*, written by the Reverend Mr. Geneste and contained in ten solid volumes. He found that between 1700 and 1830 nearly four thousand dramatic works of one kind or another were produced in England ; and he declared that of these four thousand plays of all kinds produced in the course of one hundred and thirty years, " three thousand nine hundred and fifty are absolutely unknown, except by name, to any but professed students of English dramatic literature. Of the remaining fifty, only thirty-five are ever presented on the English boards at the present day ; of these thirty - five, only seventeen are works of acknowledged literary merit ; and of these seventeen, only eleven can claim to rank as standard works." That is to say, that during the

hundred and thirty years when the drama in England, if not at its best, was at
least the centre of literary interest and
more important and more profitable than
any· other department of literature, only
once in about ten years, on an average,
was a play produced which by some union
of popular attributes with literary quality
has managed to survive to the present
day. Only one play in ten years! Since
1830 have we not seen produced on the
stage more often than once in ten years
plays worthy to survive the century and
likely to accomplish that difficult task?

We give ear to the picked plays of the
past, and we give no thought to their in-
numerable companions "all silent and all
damned." We see the comedies carefully culled by time, and we do not see
their unlovely companions all faded and
gone. We look abroad on the theatre of
our own time, and the weeds have sprung
up with the flowers, and they are far more
numerous than the flowers, and they hide
the flowers from us; and many are wont
to deny that there are any flowers at all.
But the managers of the theatres in the

year 1983 will probably find little difficulty in picking out of the ten thousand
plays produced in England and America
between 1800 and 1900 at least ten equal
in quality to the average of those which
now survive from among the plays written between 1700 and 1800.

It is not a hard task to make out a list
of the so-called " Old Comedies," and the
examination is not without interest. Mr.
Gilbert did not go further back than 1700;
and, as it happens, there is only one play
older than 1700 which still holds the stage
—except certain of Shakspere's. This one
play is the " New Way to Pay Old Debts "
of Massinger, acted at the Phœnix in
Drury Lane and published in 1633. For
seventy years after 1633 no English comedy was acted which keeps the boards
nowadays. After 1703 they come a little
more closely together; and it is perhaps
best to draw up a chronological list of
them, giving the name of the author and
the title of the comedy.

1703—Colley Cibber's " She Would and She
    Would Not."

1709—Mrs. Centlivre's " Busybody."

1717—Mrs. Centlivre's " Wonder ! a Woman
    Keeps a Secret."

1759—[Garrick's ?] " High Life Below
    Stairs."

1761—Colman's " Jealous Wife."

1762—Foote's " Liar."

1766—Garrick and Colman's " Clandestine
    Marriage."

1773—Goldsmith's " She Stoops to Conquer."

1775—Sheridan's " Rivals."

1777—Sheridan's " School for Scandal."

1779—Sheridan's " Critic ; or, a Tragedy
    Rehearsed."

1780—Mrs. Cowley's " Belle's Stratagem."

1792—Holcroft's " Road to Ruin."

1794—O'Keefe's " Wild Oats."

1797—Colman the Younger's " Heir - at-
    Law."

1801—Colman the Younger's " Poor Gentle-
    man."

1805—Colman the Younger's " John Bull."

1805—Tobin's " Honeymoon."

From 1805 to 1830 no comedy was produced of sufficient vitality to have come
down to us. But between 1830 and 1860
several plays were produced which have

been included among the "Old Comedies." These are:

1832—Knowles's "Hunchback."
1837—Knowles's "Love Chase."
1840—Bulwer's "Money."
1841—Boucicault's "London Assurance."
1844—Boucicault's "Old Heads and Young Hearts."
1852—Reade and Taylor's "Masks and Faces."
1855—Taylor's "Still Waters Run Deep."

Here, then, we have twenty-five plays written and acted between 1705 and 1855, a space of a century and a half. These are the "Old Comedies," and they are the survivors out of at least five thousand dramatic pieces of one kind or another. Of course this list of "Old Comedies" is not absolutely identical with that which would be drawn up by any other student of the stage. As a matter of fact, probably no two persons would agree on exactly the same twenty-five "Old Comedies;" nor would another writer inevitably limit the number to precisely the quarter of a hundred. Due allowance must be made for the personal equation. As yet the canon of the "Old Comedies" has not been closed and declared by any council. The present list, however, is my doxy, and I do not believe that your doxy would differ greatly from it. Any list would probably contain at least twenty of these twenty-five. And as no list can be promulgated by authority, the one given above may serve as well as another.

One of the first remarks one feels called on to make, after considering this list of "Old Comedies," is that there has been no decline and falling off in the comic drama as here represented, and that—excepting always the plays of Goldsmith and Sheridan, two exceptional dramatists—the comedies written in this century are quite equal in literary value and theatrical effect to the comedies written in the last century. Without going again into this quarrel of the ancients and moderns, it may be said safely that the five latest plays on this list are not inferior to the five earliest. Lord Lytton's "Money," Boucicault's "London Assurance" and "Old Heads and Young Hearts,"

Reade and Taylor's "Masks and Faces," and Taylor's "Still Waters Run Deep," taken together are quite as interesting a quintet as Colley Cibber's "She Would and She Would Not," Mrs. Cowley's "Busybody" and "Wonder" (Townley's or Garrick's) "High Life Below Stairs," and Colman's "Jealous Wife." Artificial as are "London Assurance" and "Old Heads and Young Hearts," they are not more artificial than "She Would and She Would Not" or the "Busybody," and they are quite as lively and as bustling and as full of the rattle and snap of epigram and equivoke. In Cibber, indeed, the characters are wholly external, and the superficial movement does not completely mask the essential emptiness; while in Jesse Rural Boucicault has drawn with many caressing and tender touches a type of simple and gentle goodness not unworthy of Goldsmith, by whom, no doubt, it was suggested. It cannot be denied that there has been of late years a falling off in the drama of poetic ideals and resolute elevation, from which the popular taste seems in some way to have turned; but it may be denied most emphatically that there has been any falling off in comedy itself.

Another remark called forth by a consideration of this list of "Old Comedies" is that although English comedy is very lively—far livelier than French, for example—fuller of bustle and gayety and far nearer to farce, it is not lacking in a substantial morality. Probably no one of these twenty-five "Old Comedies" was written with conscious moral purpose and to declare the viciousness of vice and the virtuousness of virtue; and no one of them obtrudes any other moral than the ever-admirable moral of a healthy life and of the duty of gayety and innocent mirth. Assuredly none of these comedies is fit to serve as a subject of Sunday meditation. It was Goethe in his old age who said, "It is strange that with all I have done, there is not one of my poems that would suit the Lutheran hymn-book." With the exception of Boucicault's two plays, which were the work of an old heart and a young head, and which are hard in tone and therefore not altogether wholesome, there is no one of these plays which any girl might fear taking her mother to see. There is no one of them which leaves a bad taste in the mouth. There is no one of them which will give you a troubled conscience at night or a troubled head in the morning. There is no one of them which will not give a hearty laugh and an hour of pleasant amusement.

To ask more than this is to ask too much. *Veluti in speculo* and *Castigat ridendo mores* are good enough mottoes for a drop-curtain, but they are not to be taken seriously as part of the code of criticism. We look in the mirror, and we see our neighbor's failings and our neighbor's faults. The comic writer laughingly castigates manners, and we laughingly see the lash fall on our neighbor's back. " There are now quite as many Celimènes, Alcestes, Arnolphes, and Tartuffes as there were in Molière's time," says the younger Dumas, one of the masters of modern comedy; " we each of us recognize them, but they do not recognize themselves." In other words, comedy corrects no one;

and, of a truth, correction is not the true
mission of comedy. Conceding that Shakspere's " Taming of the Shrew " never
cured a virago or Molière's " Miser " a
miser, so much the worse for the virago
and the miser ; it is enough for comedy
that it confirms the healthy in their
health. So Lessing, the foremost of German moralists, tells us ; and he adds that
Molière's " Miser " is instructive to the ex-
travagant man, and Regnard's " Game-
ster " to the man who never gambles : " the
follies they themselves have not, others
may have with whom they have to live."
Perhaps no better words can be found
with which to close this paper than those
of Lessing on this very subject : " Comedy
is to do us good through laughter, but not
through derision ; not just to counteract
those faults at which it laughs, nor simply
and solely in those persons who possess
these laughable faults. Its true general
use consists in laughter itself ; in the practice of our powers to discern the ridiculous, to discern it easily and quickly under
all cloaks of passion and fashion ; in all
admixture of good and bad qualities, even

in the wrinkles of solemn earnestness. . . .
A preservative is a valuable medicine,
and all morality has none more powerful
and effective than the ridiculous."

1883.

III.—A PLEA FOR FARCE

In one of the best edited and best written, most careful and most conscientious
newspapers in New York I read, not long
ago, a criticism of a new comedy, which
was praised as "possessing a serious as
well as a comic interest, and rarely de-
scending to the level of absolute farce."
Apparently the critic here asserts by insinuation that "absolute farce" can be
found only in the lowest levels of the
dramatic mine. A similar assumption is
frequent in current theatrical criticism,
and the theatrical critic is not seldom
moved to bemoan the decadence of the
drama as indicated by the decline of
comedy and the acceptance of farce in
its stead. The theatrical critic, it may

be remarked incidentally, generally insists on illuminating the present by the light of other days, and he is prone to cry *O tempora! O mores!* which, after all, is but the Latin for the latter-day and more logical *autre temps, autres moeurs!*

"Life," as one of Margaret Fuller's girl pupils once said, "is to laugh or cry, according to our constitution." To many, if not to most, it is nobler to cry than to laugh. The tear is more dignified than the smile. Thus tragedy claims a superiority over comedy and still more over farce. "Let a man of cheerful disposition," writes Mr. Lecky, in his *History of European Morals* (3d ed., vol. i., p. 85), seeking to prove the power of our intuitions—"let a man of cheerful disposition, and of cultivated but not very fastidious taste, observe his own emotions and the countenances of those around him during the representation of a clever tragedy and of a clever farce, and it is probable that he will come to the conclusion that his enjoyment in the latter case has been both more unmingled and more intense than in the former. He has felt no lassitude, he has not endured the amount of pain that necessarily accompanies the pleasure of pathos; he has experienced a vivid, absorbing pleasure, and he has traced similar emotions in the violent demonstrations of his neighbors. Yet he will readily admit that the pleasure derived from the tragedy is of a higher order than that derived from the farce. Sometimes he will find himself hesitating which of the two he will choose. The love of mere enjoyment leads him to the one. A sense of its *nobler* character inclines him to the other."

It would take too long to consider here at length why it is that tragedy is intuitively acknowledged to be nobler than farce; but the fact admits of no dispute. Tragedy is held to be higher than comedy, and comedy is held to be higher than farce. Perhaps a consciousness that tragedy and comedy are nobler forms of the drama is the cause that the estimation of farce is unduly low. Perhaps even the greater and more boisterous entertainment afforded by farce is the cause of the contempt in which many affect to hold it, for there is a strange tendency in mankind to despise those who amuse it, especially if the laughter excited is at all hearty and robust. A shrewd and ambitious politician never dares to be as funny as he can ; he knows that it is better to make the people take him seriously; he curbs his humor as best he may ; and rather than be hailed as a wit he is willing, by force of dulness, to attain a reputation for profundity.

Now I, for one, at least, fail to see any reason why farce should be stamped with the stigma of illegitimacy. There are degrees in the drama, no doubt, and the highest places are reserved for tragedy and for comedy; but melodrama and burlesque and farce are all legitimate dramatic forms, and they have each an honorable pedigree. Modern melodrama may recognize itself in some of the plays of Euripides and Sophocles ; and M. d'Ennery, for example, would not disavow Œdipus Rex. Burlesque may claim as its founder that great poet Aristophanes, and as one of its friends the author of "A Midsummer-Night's Dream." Farce

could trace its descent from Menander
and from Plautus, if it needed to go further back than the authors of the " Merry
Wives of Windsor" and the " Précieuses
Ridicules."

One of the phenomena of theatrical
history is the scarcity of comedy and the
prevalence of farce. There has been no
time recorded in the annals of the English stage when the critics were not com-
plaining of the dearth of real comedy, and
denouncing the plethora of farce. As we
look along the list of old comedies which
keep the stage to this day, we find a very
large proportion of farces. What are
"She Would and She Would Not," "The
Country Girl" and " The Busybody" but
farces? Goldsmith's enemies denounced
" She Stoops to Conquer" as farce, and
declared that some of its incidents were
too low even for that. Sheridan's friends
cannot deny that a good half at least of
" The Rivals" is frank farce—and, in fact,
it is the better half. And as for the
" Heir-at-Law"—with which Mr. Jefferson and Mr. Florence have been delight-
ing us of late, and which many theatrical

critics have been as prompt to praise as
they would be swift to condemn were any
living author to bring forth such a het-
erogeny of absurdities—Colman's farrago
of oddity and commonplace is farce, if it
is anything at all. In fact, it is difficult
to deny the frequent exactness of the
epigram declaring that "a comedy is a
farce by an author who is dead."

The only play of contemporary English
life which Shakspere wrote, the "Merry
Wives of Windsor," is a farce, and not a
very good farce either. The one play
which he borrowed from a Latin dramatist, the "Comedy of Errors," is a farce,
and not a very good farce. The best of
Shakspere's farces is the "Taming of
the Shrew," which has a contagion of
humor and a swing of movement lacking
in the others, despite their rapidity and
their bustle. Of all the last-century
stage-versions of Shakspere the most
tolerable is Garrick's "Katherine and Pe-
truchio." The only other farces of that
century which rival it are the delightful
"High Life Below Stairs" (which Garrick
probably wrote) and the "Critic" (which

was written by Sheridan, Garrick's successor in the management of Drury Lane Theatre, and which drove from the stage the earlier farce on which it was founded, the "Rehearsal," of the Duke of Buckingham).

In the last half of the present century not a few of the best of our plays are farces, and though we may think lightly of those who make us laugh, surely we ought to be grateful to Mr. Bronson Howard for "Saratoga," to Mr. Gilbert for "Engaged," to Mr. Grundy for the "Snowball, " and to Mr. Pinero for the "Magistrate." Two of the greatest successes of the British stage in the past score of years have been " Pink Dominos," an adaptation of a French farce, and the "Private Secretary," an adaptation of a German farce. Three of the greatest successes of the American stage in the same period have been Mr. Daly's "Big Bonanza," "7-20-8," and "A Night Off," all three of them adapted from German farces.

In the French theatre farce has been as prolific and as popular as in ours. A

14

very large proportion of Molière's best
work took the form of farce. "Les Précieuses Ridicules," the "Médecin Mal-
gré Lui," the "Malade Imaginaire," the
"Étourdi," "Monsieur de Pourceaugnac"
—what are all these but farces?—and the
"Bourgeois Gentilhomme" is perilously
close to it. The comic plays of Regnard
are called comedies, and as such apparently
they are accepted by the French; but most
of them and the best of them are farce—
exuberant, robustious, and inordinately
funny farce. Could any one ever be in
doubt whether the "Légataire Universel"
was comedy or farce? And in the two
great comedies of Beaumarchais, the
"Barbier de Séville" and the "Mariage de
Figaro," there is more than a mere infusion of farce; certain acts are super-
saturated with it. In this century, Scribe
and M. Sardou have written farces as they
have written plays of every other sort;
and in its day "Oscar; ou, Le Mari qui
trompe sa Femme" was as risky and as
broadly humorous as was "Divorçons" a
generation later. And lives there a man
with soul so dead and so impervious to

humor as not to dissolve into laughter at
the sight of the "Panache" of Gondinet,
of the "Boule" and the "Tricoche et
Cacolet" of MM. Meilhac and Halévy, and
of the "Chapeau de paille d'Italie," the
"Cagnotte" and the "Trente Millions de
Gladiator" of Labiche?

Surely a form of art which can show as
long a roll of masterpieces as farce is not
despicable. Surely it deserves to be
treated with the respect paid to the other
forms of the drama. It is not as difficult,
perhaps, as comedy, which depends on
the clash of character and the sparkle of
epigram; but it is not easy. It is an art
with laws of its own. It is not burlesque,
for one thing, although it is akin to
burlesque; and a marriage between the
two is within the forbidden degrees.

Like true burlesque, as distinguished
from mere extravaganza, farce demands
the utmost seriousness in its conception
and in its performance. Garrick declared
that comedy was a serious thing — he
would not have denied that farce is even
more serious. Farce is negative towards
burlesque and positive towards comedy;

it repels the one and attracts the other. While farce and burlesque are abhorrent and cannot be joined to advantage, farce and comedy combine readily and melt one into the other in vague and imperceptible fluctuations. The farcical-comedy is not only a legitimate form of art, but it is almost inevitable, as we learn by looking down the long vista of the drama and seeing how very often it has blossomed luxuriantly. The bastard hybrid called " farce-comedy," prevalent of late in our theatres—a queer medley of various kinds of entertainment, musical, saltatorial, pantomimic, and even acrobatic—may be often clever, but it is rarely either farce or comedy.

In the history of literature, as in natural history, advancing science has shown us that there are no hard and fast lines between species and genera, but insensible gradations from one to the other, with scarcely a missing link anywhere. Farce bears much the same relation to comedy that melodrama does to tragedy. In farce and in melodrama there is a more summary psychology than in com-

edy and in tragedy. Events are of more
importance than the persons to whom
they happen. The author seeks to interest the spectator rather in things than
in men and women; he relies more on
the force of situation than on the development of character.

Mr. William Archer (the one critic of
the acted drama in England who is
worthy to be named with M. Francisque
Sarcey, the chief critic of the acted drama
in France) says that "melodrama may
be defined as illogical tragedy, in which
causes and effects are systematically dis-
proportionate, and the hero is the plaything of special providences." So farce
may be defined as an ultra-logical comedy, in which everything is pushed to ex-
tremes, and the hero is the plaything of
special providences. In farce, for instance, we see a fibster involving himself
in unending snarls, and yet in the end
getting off scot-free. And the moral of
the play is not in the happy ending
brought about arbitrarily and as the dramatist please; it resides rather in the hearty
laughter which has cleared the air, and

which is a boon in itself and a gift to be thankful for. Laughter is the great antiseptic; and it is quick to kill the germs of unwholesome sentimentality by which comedy is often attacked.

But laughter is a gift for which mankind is rarely as grateful as it ought to be. We are eager to find distraction rom worry and surcease of sorrow if only for a moment, and we are ready to pay the humorist the wages he asks. Yet oddly enough, we are often ashamed of our own laughter, and we are prone to visit this qualm of conscience upon the author of our amusement. Farce is a natural and useful form of the drama; it reckons many a masterpiece; and to make it bear the bar sinister is unkind and unfair.

1890.

THE END